ELEMENTS OF ART EXPERIENCE

by

ALAN D RILEY

The Elements of Art Experience
Published by Alan D Riley
Kenmore, WA
Copyright © 2018 by the author. All rights reserved.

COPYRIGHT NOTICE

Please be advised that the writings and images in this book are subject to a royalty. They are fully protected under the copyright laws of the United States of America, and of all countries covered by the International Copyright Union (including the Dominion of Canada and the rest of the British Commonwealth), and of all countries covered by the Pan-American Copyright Convention and the Universal Copyright Convention, and of all countries with which the United States has reciprocal copyright relations. All rights, including professional, amateur, motion picture, recitation, lecturing, public reading, radio broadcasting, television, video or sound recording, all other forms of mechanical or electronic reproduction, information storage and retrieval systems and photocopying, and the rights of translation into foreign languages, are strictly reserved. Particular emphasis is laid upon the question of public readings, permission for which must be secured from the Author's agent in writing.

Foreword

The Elements of Art Experience was completed in 1964. It began as an attempt to answer the question, "What is an art experience?" for my own use as an artist and art teacher. I had no intent to publish my conclusions in any form, but once into the complications that arise from such a fundamental question, I learned I would also have to address related issues that surrounded the art experience to entirely understand it.

What began as a compilation of notes ended up as this short book. With no immediate plans to share it, I put it away to think about. Life sweeps us along in multiple directions. Other pressing issues seemed more important. Maybe others would come to similar conclusions and insights. Maybe they would do it better, relieving me of the duty of entering my study into the public discourse.

These hopes have not proven to be the case. I do feel an obligation to present this work to others who are profoundly moved by works of art and who do not find art experience demeaned by a close examination of its elements. Now ninety years old, I find myself too diminished in both mental agility and memory to bring its scholarship up to date. Yet I do believe this work still stands as useful in that vital discussion about art and its importance in culture. I leave the reader to decide.

– Alan D Riley

CONTENTS

The Divided Mind   7

The Elements of Art Experience   24

Art and Society   45

Art and the Public School   54

Art and Morality   67

About the Author   79

THE DIVIDED MIND

Discussions of philosophers, artists, teachers, psychologists, writers and sociologists converge with an unusual degree of regularity upon a single issue of contemporary Western life: the division in humankind's conception of itself and the society it forms, between intuitive or subjective, and rational or objective modes of mental response. Each contributor to the discussion brings one's own terms and direction in related sets of opposing twos, all of which are, by now, quite familiar to us; body and mind, heart and mind, sensual and logical, insight and intellect, inner directed and outer directed, haptic and visual, divergent and convergent, spontaneous and deliberate, introvert and extrovert.

The content and aims of the conceptions mentioned here present a wide variety of development and scope. But all are consistent in one important respect: they subscribe to the proposition that mental response may best be described as taking place somewhere between two unlike processes of mind. Some theorists see these opposing two qualities mingling or fusing, others see them as distinct organizations which function together only as complements. In all cases a consistent implication emerges: western civilization harbors a strong tendency to entertain a concept of mental process which separates intuitive and rational responses into two recognizable entities, one of which represents deeply felt subjective awareness and the other, objective agreed upon facts, rules, theories, and mores.

The presence of this division in so entrenched it is difficult now to discuss mind and its processes and predilections without resorting to the use of opposite twos, if only for purpose of illustration. The split is carried by society at large to the individuals within it. They, in turn, embody the predisposition and biases which perpetuate the separation of intuition and rationality and cause the split to endure.

It is not possible to discuss art experience or examine its elements without taking into account the force of this tendency. It will be the purpose of this chapter to document its existence, examine its causes and effects and lay out the possibilities and limitations of this division's influence as it extends into the art experience.

    Katherine Gilbert and Helmut Kuhn state in their book, *A History of Esthetics*, that we have "an ancient quarrel between philosophy and poetry because both wished to claim exclusive possession of truth." We have written evidence of such a clash as far back as the Fifth and Sixth Centuries B.C., in Greece.

    In *The Republic*, Plato made a distinction between the world of intellect and the world of the senses which has influenced us profoundly. According to his view, what our senses tell us is untrue unless our knowledge of truth, guided by intellect, was so sure that we could have an extrasensory vision permitting us to the see reality itself. There would be no room for the vague imaginings of a poet or artist. Free inquiry must direct itself toward the ideal of absolute reality. We cannot trust our senses. The images they provide are limited by our ability to perceive and discriminate. The touch of wisdom present in Plato's argument in not sufficient to counteract an effect on our recognition and use of sensual imagery; proprioception as well as perception. One who considers the ideal world more real than their cold, hunger, immediate joy or terror, denies a wide range of information and experience.

    In his discussion of Plato's theory of immortality, Bertrand Russell has said in *A History of Western Philosophy*, "Liberations from the tyranny of the body contributes to greatness, but just as much to greatness in sin as to greatness in virtue."

    Examining the historical background for the theories of opposing twos, Siegfried Marck writes in the section on dialectical materialism from the *History of Philosophical Systems*, "What then, does 'dialectical' mean? Immediately the name Hegel (1770-1831) comes to our mind. By no means was Hegel the inventor of this type of thinking. It has had a long history which in Western philosophy began with Heraclitus (536-470 B.C.). Hegel said there was no sentence of Heraclitus which he would not have been able to include in his own logic. In a different way, Zeno (490-430 B.C.) of the anti-Heraclitean Eleatic School developed dialects, and still another type of dialectics was represented by Plato (427-347 B.C.). These different forms of dialectics have something in common: they are characterized by the central role of the opposites and contradictions for both human thinking as well as for reality."

The advent of Christianity brought with it an increasing intensity of moral tone which, attached as it was to all issues from metaphysics to trade, added moral implications to each question. Henceforth, personal responses would always be examined in the light of virtue as it existed relatively in this world and absolutely in the next. The terms of the struggle were clear; humankind's instinct for passion and original disposition for sin against the strength of its faith to deny these. The propensity for duality was enhanced by a total concept which divided the world into the forces of darkness and forces of light. The effect of the struggle is equally clear. For twelve centuries, man comforted himself in the confines of a powerful, if narrow, faith which encouraged him to accept instead of question and answer instead of ask.

From trade and acquisition of wealth by persons outside government and the church, new forces emerged which required renewed inquiry and greater exposure to other cultures and differing points of view. Gradually the specific powers of the church weakened, but for some time, its influence did not, for now its general theology was carried forward by more powerful individuals and nations with great resources at their command. In a final analysis, the effect of reopening inquiry would overwhelm the geographical expansion of a growing Christian influence and, in part, that inquiry was itself furthered by the Reformation within church influence. But while one segment of Christianity encouraged inquiry and the larger portion discouraged, it, there was common agreement about the essentials: man was born in sin; his natural impulses and sensual appetite must be curbed to make way for higher passions which must be taught and learned through rational and intellective channels.

Perhaps Descartes embodied the dual conflict more precisely than anyone else among theological thinkers. When he proclaimed, "I think, therefore I am", he demonstrated clearly the pull of both interests. The statement would have been equally forceful, if not equally consequential, had he chosen to select another verb than "think", – I feel, I sense, I know – were alternatives which he very likely considered and rejected. Yet we remember his admitting that the heart has reasons of its own which the head will never understand.

Throughout history's record, the duality continued. Thoreau, after enrapturing the virtues and delights of external sensuality in his discussion of Higher Laws from *Walden*, finds sensuality repugnant as it applies to his internal requirement. Despite his ability to absorb so much from life around him, he could not escape the broad prejudice of his time; immediate needs to sustain and enjoy life are, at best, to be distrusted: at worst, disgusting.

Thomas De Quincy, from his essay *On the Knocking at the Gate in MacBeth*, writes: "Here I pause for one moment, to exhort the reader never to pay any attention to his understanding, when it stands in opposition to any other faculty of his mind. The mere understanding, however useful and indispensable, is the meanest faculty in the human mind, and the most to be distrusted, and yet the great majority of people trust to nothing else, which may do for ordinary life, but not for philosophical purposes."

Goethe attempts to handle one part of the same apparent conflict when he writes to Schiller in the spring of 1801: "I hold that whatever genius is done as genius is done unconsciously. The man of genius can act according to reason when convinced by reflection, but all that is incidental. No work of genius can be improved or freed from its faults by reflection and its immediate results. But reflection and action may so improve a man of genius that he ends by producing exemplary works."

Henri Bergson picks up the same issue and makes a sharp distinction between instinct and intellect thereby reinforcing the ancient dichotomy and inspiring many excursions of art and social science into the spheres of pure life.

John Unterecker, in writing of W.B. Yeats in his *Readers' Guide To Yeats*, mentions that the poet saw all human life as a mingling of opposites. In his book, *A Vision*, Yeats drew a diagram of two intersecting cones. One represented solar man who was moral, objective, factual, space oriented, and dependent upon physical things. The other was lunar man, who was time oriented, aesthetic, and subjective. Lunar man responds according to emotions.

Clive Bell, in his book *Art*, tends to divide people into two camps when they are confronted by, or engaged in, the production of art objects. On one hand he posits those who will settle for art as a specific communicative device based upon externals of the object.

On the other, are those who perceive through form and respond to rhythm or felt realities.

D.H. Lawrence devotes and entire section of his *Twilight in Italy* to the construction of a two pole understanding of one's personal role with respect to his or her own creativity and self-belief. He describes Europe as populated by a Northerner and a Southerner. Through a series of intricately related two part divisions, he follows their separate paths from the Renaissance to create a progression of character by opposites, one of which is objective, calculating and cool, the other subjective, spontaneous and warm. He sees two ever opposing dichotomies: "Two infinite, negative and positive, they are always related but they are never identical. They are always opposite but there exists a relationship between them."

In his essay *Men Must Work and Women as Well*, Lawrence takes up the same theme. "Now we are all basically and permanently physical. So is the earth, so even is the air. What then, is going to be the result of all this recoil and repulsion, which our civilization has deliberately fostered? The result is really only one and the same; some form of collective social madness." He goes on to reset the condition and project a solution. "A great part of society is irreparably lost: abstracted into non-physical, mechanical entities whose motive power is still recoil, repulsion, revulsion, hate, and ultimately, blind destruction. It only remains for some men and women individuals, to try to get back their bodies and preserve the other flow of warmth, affection, and physical union. There is nothing else to do."

Carl Jung's two contradictory major tendencies in his extrovert-introvert conception are also related to the intuitive-rational split. The extrovert is more comfortable and adept at coping with objective circumstances, the introvert responds primarily to subjective circumstances; his own conception and feelings. Jung points out that these tendencies are not dichotomous and states that most people share both tendencies and become ambiverts. While it would be inaccurate to squeeze Jung's conception wholesale into the ancient heritage of division, the resemblance is evident.

Lowenfeld's haptic-visual system is a direct descendent sans moral implications. The primary division remains intact: subjective and intuitive as opposed to objective and rational.

Burkhart's formulation of spontaneous and deliberate modes of thinking and E. Paul Torrance's divergent and convergent tendencies stem from the same family tree. While their differences and important contributions will not be discussed here, it should be noted that these last three systems also hold in common the position taken by Jung: the two poles of each tendency represent extremes. Most individuals share each tendency simultaneously in varying degrees of balance.

In his work *Art As Experience*, John Dewey recognizes the division and illuminates it in the following way: "Why is there repulsion when the high achievements of fine art are brought into connection with common life, the life that we share with all living creatures? Why is life thought of as an affair of low appetite, or at best, a thing of gross sensation, and ready to sink from its best to the level of lust and harsh cruelty? A complete answer to the question would involve the writing of a history of morals that would set for the conditions that have brought about contempt for the body, fear of the senses, and the opposition of flesh to spirit."

Dewey suggests one explanation in the following statement: "Since sense organs, with their connected motor apparatus, are the means of…participation, any and every derogation of them, whether practical or theoretical is at one effect and cause of a narrowed and dulled life experience. Oppositions of mind and body, soul and matter, spirit and flesh, all have their origins fundamentally, in fear of what life may bring forth. They are marks of contraction and withdrawal."

Jacques Barzun, in *The House of Intellect*, makes it clear that we hold the intellect to be non-sensual and, in a sense, antagonistic to physical life. "It is enough that intellectual work enforces sedentary habits – that intellect shuns the outdoors to coop itself up in a house – to suggest an antagonism between it and the free exercise of the body that seems to typify life." Becoming more specific, he later points out: "The deep, universal distrust of intellect rests upon its hostility to what is felt as the pulse of life. Common language records this opposition in a dozen ways: life warm, hot, glowing; intellect is cold and dull – intellect stands on the margin of existence and convinces, if at all, by the roundabout road of argument – words in place of acts. Any pair of common images about the two shows them as antagonists – intellect, stiff, angular, unchanging; life flowing and adaptive."

Barzun later observes: "Indeed, the ultimate perceptions of life are not only not demonstrable, they defy communication. If it were possible to talk to the unborn, one could never explain to them how it feels to be alive, for life is washed in the speechless real. And, conversely, whoever checks the sense of life by always preferring ideas and words grows blind to realities."

The house of intellect is indeed divided when Barzun tells us: "Intellect tends automatically to undermine, or at least, to counterbalance the effect of art: at the source intellect discusses the concrete particular, reducing it to an instance of the general; and in the product – the work of art – intellect either challenges with stubborn literalness its evocative and richly ambiguous assertions, or when baffled by the calm self-sufficiency of the object, it asks, as the philosopher did about the sonata, 'what does it prove?'"

In the seeming deadlock between life and art versus organized thought, Barzun asks: "Which are we to choose, believe, follow?"

In his discussion of the scientific method as it applies to aesthetics from his book *Toward Science in Aesthetics*, Thomas Munro reminds us that elementary philosophy students learn that the red rose they see may not be precisely the same red rose as others see. Munro concludes: "Yet that ultimate doubt is of no practical or scientific consequence whatever." This despite the certainty that the possibility of any fact is what the endeavor of science is all about.

Throughout the history of Western people and civilization mankind has created, the split has endured; sometimes it is made explicit, but usually it is an underlying assumption widely held and rarely disapproved of. Its forms vary and its terms change, but its theme remains – there are two parts to living experience. One is objective, rational, practical, and dependable. The other is subjective, intuitive, impractical, and mysterious. For many hundreds of years each was associated clearly in countless religious documents and secular writings with a moral value. The first experience was useful and represented the full road of enlightenment and possibility. The second was dark, passionate, and permeated with the sin inherited from an ancient temptation. Rational inquiry and the freedom not to believe has not yet freed us from the imposition of a long held, and deeply felt prejudice. Psychologists and artists themselves in our time, have assumed that since art is charged with the mysteries of irrational passion, it must be created by pathological states of mind or states of mind which represent a defense against a mental condition we could not otherwise cope with.

Charles Lamb, C.B. Shaw, and Lionel Trilling have all found it necessary to mount a specific defense for art against these assertions. It is understandable that we have come to associate sensitivity with art and both with madness. One may ask, does mental illness make its victims more sane than those who escape it? But the popular reply might be, only in areas which have no practical consequence.

Of the many influential figures emerging from the secularization of morality, two of the most important in our recent past are Karl Marx and Sigmund Freud. Both recognized an indifferent environment and defied the tyranny of religious obedience shared by their fellows. Both substituted sharp inquiry for unquestioning faith; Freud approaching society from the individual's own interior struggle with society's modifications and severe requirements, and Marx from society's conflict between classes over the distribution of wealth. It is not surprising that each created a mechanism for comprehending the forces they considered to be most compelling, which ignored or denigrated the value of sensual and intuitive sources of regeneration, knowledge and possibility.

Perhaps it is too easy to point to the ills of contemporary life to find supporting evidence; too easy because the temptations to include so much cannot be offset by any degree of certainty, and too easy because our list of violations against the eyes, the ears, the note, the tongue, and the sense of touch would stretch to volumes. Suffice it to say that Ananda K. Coomaraswamy, in *Christian and Oriental Philosophy of Art*, has presented considerable evidence for his conclusion that, in the western world, we have, for the first time in history, created an industry without art. Perhaps it would be more accurate to say that we have created an entire culture without the ability or interest to maintain art and art is being thrust aside to make room for entertainment – a quicker, easier substitute.

We did not consciously intend this to happen. We were looking toward other directions. The new power of technology and science which promised so much and provided so much, has fascinated us and captured nearly all of our attentions and effort. It has taken the place of the church in matters of faith. The new miracles will come from science. Many believe it is God's way of providing them, thus having the benefits of two faces of faith's coin and thus holding fast to the most powerful source of prejudice against intuition and sensuality which can be identified.

    We must ask the question, has a culture which lofts rationality and objectivity at the expense of passion and subjectivity created and an improvement in the quality of life? We must also ask what one means by the phrase 'quality of life'. Our material gains are immense. Our attention to science has been profitable. But what has it cost in matters of spirit? We have made financial progress on a large scale. We have made it possible for more people to live and to live longer. These are substantial achievements. But have we made life a better experience? We cannot clearly answer this crucial question, but that is less important than the fact that we seldom find it asked.

    The problem of examining this condition is obviously much easier than distinguishing causes. It involves the risky business of analyzing conditions so accurately that one can argue back to precedent conditions and identify the rise of particular influences with respect both to time and force, and evaluate that influence upon all of the phenomena following it. Such a route is fraught with hazards, but no alternatives are available. We will proceed with more regard for possibilities than for caution.

    When we consider the state of mind which we respond to as children and the alterations of that state as society imposes its requirements upon us, it is less difficult to appreciate the primitive inclination to reduce complex matters to two opposing forces at work upon the same object or within the same area. We begin as infants with sensuous apprehension. Our first condition is subjective and entirely self-referent. All of our existence is a response to sensed intuitive need. It is first, primary, fundamental, but not adequate to provide access to a society which depends upon cooperation and requires that need gratification be made understandable and be withheld until a propitious time.

    From our early moments of existence we begin the long conflict between our immediate needs and society's interest in directing and objectifying our need into a useful part of a larger cooperative effort to survive. There is a constant cumulative pressure which forces the outer objective condition upon our consciousness. We learn our language, mores, history, identity, and possibility from the wisdom of the tribe. That learning teaches us to selectively deny what we learn others will not believe in nor approve of. Our denial of disparate or individual, subjective responses makes it clear that we should distrust the intuitive source of information and experience. Cooperative living requires the sacrifice of subjective responses to objective conditions. It is a first step all of us take toward the tendency to examine conflict or tension as the result of two opposing forces, but it goes beyond this by inveighing a deeply ingrained moral implication and practical guide calculated to last a lifetime. That conflict creates a sense of value concerning subjective and objective responses which will extend to every new experience the well-integrated individual will encounter.

It is not the purpose of this work to attempt a final evaluation of the conflict but merely to examine it and distill from it what is pertinent to the elements of art and the experience of art. Presumable, somewhere in the conflict lies a golden mean for each individual. It would represent a theoretical position and line of action which embodies the finest balance between the attributes of intuitive and rational knowledge. It would fluctuate with particular capacities and needs and the state and nature of society. But we cannot ignore that the first lesson is also the longest and the last. And woe be to him who would ignore it!

Does the division of private versus public interest conform to, or create an actual division within the mind? The most influential and clearly defined framework for our heritage slips aside from the question by using the concept of soul. We are said to be possessed of the evil or possessed by the power of salvation through belief in God. Religion, in general, and Christianity in particular, has contributed a mighty arm in support of social order. It is an original law giver from which civil order in western society has largely developed. Its sanction is essential. Man is born in sin. He succumbed to temptation and is evil. He will be punished with eternal torture unless he believes he is evil and is willing to repent his original sin through belief itself.

The conflict between private and public interest must be solved to the advantage of public interest or society will fail. Christianity, accepting the duty of all religious systems, made failure to respond to God's law, punishable with unimaginable horrors. Until recently, the translation each of us understands to exist between God's law and society's law was so slight that it was of no interest to anyone but scholars and clergymen. The effect of Christian belief on the conflict between subjective and objective response is clear. Believe what you are told, not what you feel. Passion and subjectivity may only play a carefully prescribed part in life. By itself, intuition is not only undependable and unimportant, it is evil, and as all good men agree, will lead to eternal damnation. All children, regardless of their station must be educated to the point where they will understand the word of God and man, for they are born in sin and must learn to resist the evil inherent in their uneducated impulses. Deny the body. It is the vehicle of sin to which the soul is exposed in temporal life.

  Organized religion began losing its dominion as soon as the secular order it fostered overwhelmed Christian power in the pursuit of its own interests of trade and culture. The Reformation added a new impetus to its lessening role. It worked both for and against the sacred influence. Today the Christian religion has lost much in that regard and stands to lose considerably more. Its reentrance into secular matters is recognition of that fact. The quality of belief is, of course, very different now than it was for so many centuries. Members of the church maintain private views at odds with official doctrine, and do so without apparent fear of damnation. We hear now about people behaving "naturally", as if this were a new condition. We imagine we are better acquainted with ourselves and the deeper mysteries of our impulses are said to become more available in the belief of an unconscious. We are groping back toward something we lost, but the emptiness and denial are still supported by the church and the societies which arose with it. The trip back will be a long one.

  It would not be possible in this discussion to make a comprehensive appraisal of man's attempt to free himself from the confines of rigidly prescribed doctrine. Trades, artists, scientists and adventurers all played a part. But in the world of ideas which has for so long been dominated by the written word and symbol, it was the rational and objective thinker, perhaps inspired by the strength and spirit of new achievements in art by more intuitive men, who recorded the acts which ultimately would destroy the unchallenged authority of the church. Spinoza, Galileo, Bacon, Lewuenhoueck, Hume, Comte, Liebniz, Darwin and others demonstrated the power of systematic observation of the world about them. New advances came more rapidly. The universe seemed headed toward a rational explanation. Poets and artists picked up the sense of new possibility and amplified it. We had developed wonderful tools which provided measurable benefits. Theory and practice applied to real objects yielded tangible results. Was the "other man" of intuition and subjective interest freed? Perhaps, in those cases where the man of science came to the point where one imagines and guesses from the paraphernalia stored in mind and bone. But once more an important phase of history which had immeasurable influence came in such a way at such a time that the prejudice against intuition and subjectivity was bolstered with a new reinforcement.

      Trade interests and governments came to appreciate the advantages offered and the age of technology began. Simply to list the remarkable accomplishments of the last hundred years in science would take volumes. Steam, electricity, hydroelectric, gas, diesel, and atomic power were harnessed to the demands of the assembly line: mass market and mass communications, prosperity, and physical health increased the number of people alive and increased the length of their lives. We live more comfortably and with less pain. How can anyone doubt the efficiency and wisdom of displacing mysterious and undependable passion with the objective, dependable virtues of logical, rational knowledge and experience? Is there even an issue to discuss? Should grown people waste their talents protecting impulses they found important as children?

      Two outstanding results of our technological advance must be pointed out. We have greatly increased the population of the world. There is considerable speculation about maintaining an ability to care for ourselves at present. The rate of growth increases, and with it, the dangers we must face confronted with such masses. The second point relates directly to the first: We require increased communication between peoples to coordinate the cooperation necessary to survival. Specifically this means that each of us lives in a world which becomes increasingly complicated. To avoid war, maintain sales, production, government, employment, trade, transportation, education, welfare, defense, and construction we need to catch people's attention more often and to hold it longer. We need to lengthen forms and create more documents with more specific information. We need to group together tighter and spend more time traveling in jammed traffic. We make smaller decisions of an ever increasing specificity. We make many more of them because we encounter more people and more changes in procedure to serve trade and communicate with more people. This trend may be inevitable, but its effect on mind and the possibility of mind's total experience is damaging. The final effect is to require a more complicated, more complete, and ever increasing rate of objective, rationally oriented responses. The ancient preference would view this as a valuable transformation since it serves to further restrict and cancel out irrelevant emotional equivalents to the business of life.

The mere existence of large numbers of people and the massive communications they require to subsist constitute an invasion of privacy which we must expect to increase. We are already so busy with the complications of coping with interruptions, rumors, new information, new forms of procedure, that life has become a constant flow or eruptions to which we can only respond with mechanical reflexes. To respond fully is impossible. We no longer have time to ask ourselves what it is we feel. Enjoying sensually the affairs of living is largely out of the question. We are too busy trying to maintain our balance against new and unexpected thrusts. We do not ask what it is we are doing. All we know is that we must do it. If we ask people what they want from life they look stunned as if the question had never occurred to them, at least not since they had become adults.

One of the unhappy benefits of the rational surge, then, is that society requires us to manipulate our desires and skills to conform to an ever tighter pattern of its needs. Society's need looms larger and larger each year in proportion to individual fulfillment. The individual must work harder at handling the detail of survival responsibilities. One must spend more time responding to outside stimulation and less time recognizing and meeting their own needs.

Once more we must ask: Is the mind actually divisible, sharing two distinct processes which conform to the terms of the ancient predisposition? Research scientist John C. Sheehan, speaking to the topic *Creative Mind and Method* for the W.G.B.H. Educational Foundation has this to say:

"One of the popular misconceptions is that science is simply complete logic; that all the conclusions follow inevitably from the situation, from the known data. There is a very real part in science for something from the individual scientist to be added which is not apparent or inherent in the situation. In other words, there is a considerable part which might be called 'art' in science, in which the individual is able to express some of his own personality, find an outlet for his artistic impulses; and this is a very much underrated role of science.

"All of science, or all of human endeavor perhaps, can be divided into two types, one the purely logical, and the other that art of the personality involved. The latter would call for more intuition, more imagination. The first part in its extreme, at least, could possibly be handled by a machine. The second part presumably never could.

"You try to go as far as possible by purely logical thinking but in any difficult problem one reaches a point where one can go no further by straight logic; or at least, it is not apparent how one can do so. Someone has commented that the scientist, the best scientist, must be able to reach the right conclusions on the basis of inadequate information or data; that is where this flash of inspiration might conceivable come in."

Sheehan's discussion demonstrates how difficult it is even to talk about a rational versus intuitive quality. Like Barzun and Dewey and Coomaraswamy, he would bring the two parts into a closer unity and senses how necessary each is to the other. Finally he suggests how they may fuse in an as yet unknown fashion to make an imaginative leap over inadequate or missing information.

It is likely that the mystery of contradiction which has seemed to exist actually lies in our ancient prejudice which severs and forever separates the sensual, physical and intuitive imagery from the logical, rational, systematic development of imagery. Because one or the other of these approaches to the idea is apparently dominant in a given effort, we conclude they operate at the expense of, and to the exclusion of, each other. They appear to be opposite and even hostile sources of awareness. Perhaps we maintain this division in the same spirit which persuades us to see rather clearly defined entities in the conscious and unconscious realms of mental process.

But examination suggests that mind operates at great depths with a wide and baffling array of approaches and sources. Some artists, convinced that the moment of solution is unplanned, are undoubtedly correct – for themselves. Others insist that it arrives right on time, in a logically developed progression of steps. Who is to say that art is built and known from only one particular source of ideation? It is, at least, both of the approaches mentioned and a great many more. When we speak of mental activity in art or any endeavor as intuitive, we describe the nature of it, not at the exclusion of logical process, but in connection with logical processes. It is no surprise that art can result from both of these emphases for they are not alien nor opposed. Finally, mental activity, as a process, cannot be profitably divided into two camps. When we do so we fail to recognize, explore, and liberate the rich complexity of possibility with which mind deals. We are waylaid by the original conflict all of us felt and continue to feel between our first state of sensual gratification and the demand to modify and deny it which society must inevitable impose. Until we appreciate the profound influence of this conflict and make peace with our own resolution of its results, it is likely to remains as a primitive bias which will cause us to ignore finer distinctions in many areas where we confront unknowns.

The forms and sequence of very powerful influences in combination with the conflict we experience as we adjust to society's larger demand has provided a long and consistent history for bias against sensual, intuitive sources of awareness. The division is not supported by evidence, but it endures and we still entertain it. Moral implications which have been attached to it add to its force even though they are inappropriate. Throughout the rest of this work we will have occasion many time to refer to this division. It has become influential in public life and has a particularly significant relationship to the art experience. But the point of view taken in this work is that the division is real only in the sense that we believe and act on it.

Two points come to mind which should be reviewed before we leave this aspect of our discussion. We have assumed that intellect and intuition are both single aspects of many more which could be said to make up descriptions of the way our mental processes operate. They penetrate, fuse and connect in such a manner that we cannot consider them as distinct properties. But we have recognized the two part conflict between private and public interests which begins at the early moments of our lives. We have also stated that private interests are subjective and intuitive and are often in opposition to the objective, external, rational condition public interest commands us to accept.

We take the view that it would be more useful for us to look upon intellect as one enlargement of mental powers. Intellect describes one's ability to adapt and maneuver in coping with our environment. It grows with experience and protects us from responding in an infantile manner, only, to the immediate sensual hungers which so dominate our earliest responses. Sensual needs thrust themselves forward. Intellect ameliorates, qualifies, and elaborates. To defend our sense of wellbeing, we become partners with society's interest; learn to defer passing needs, and create strategy. Experience teaches us what to seek and what to avoid. It acknowledges rules and attempts to locate universals. Intellect would seem to protect our subjectivity and intuition; *not* substitute for it, and *not* deny it. Intuition and felt body conditions are the very center of joy and revulsion, exaltation and despair. If we take the view that intellect is an enlargement of mental power to protect our survival interests, it is no longer necessary to consider it as a total process separate from the sensuality and antagonistic to sensuality's impulses.

It is easy to seize hold of the convenient handle of opposing twos. We live in an environment of day and night, hot and cold, right and left, up and down, stillness and motion, sun and moon, and remember the struggle it took to develop the science of light, vector analysis, mathematics, of acceleration and change, astronomy and probability. We remember encountering people who require emotional equivalents for learning experience. They have difficulty understanding or retaining information which is provided second hand. Unless they learn by first hand acquaintance with the material or the actual use of sets of symbols as applied to visible situations with visible results, they appear to be nearly incapable of learning. On the other hand we know people who comfortably accept abstract conditions surrounding symbols. For them the word or number or diagram seem to suffice. Is there a distinction worth considering between first hand learners and second hand learners? How tempting it would be to lay out a case for opposing twos. It behooves us to resist that temptation and realize that mind itself is far too complex to justify that ancient bias.

THE ELEMENTS OF ART EXPERIENCE

Art is an esthetic experience under particular and specific conditions. It takes place when a viewer invests in an object, made for the occasion of such an experience, with his or her own imagination and senses new possibilities about the condition of one's existence. It is a sensed imagery; intuition and rationality together form a momentary order of new understanding. Every art experience reorders attitudes and expectations. It is a partial remaking of one's own life. An art experience differs from a chance esthetic experience in that it requires the existence of an object which was contrived in order to bring it about.

The unity of intuitive and rational processes is inherent in the mind of man, but only the esthetic moment can fulfill it. That moment arrives as both a perception and an investment. The occurrence of an art experience, dependent as it is upon both an object and a viewer, varies widely from individual to individual. It is subject to three main influences: the influence of broad regional or national culture, the influence of education, experience, and capacity of the viewer within his own culture, and the influence of time and change as it surrounds the viewer and object with new historical contexts.

We may think of the art experience as a triangle. At the apex of the triangle is the creator or artist, and on base corner is the object the creator or creators make, at the other base corner is the viewer who responds to the object. The area within the triangle can be thought of as an art experience:

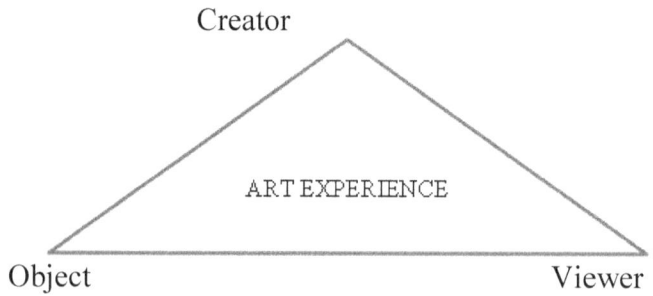

The art experience exists when the viewer, confronted by an object which stimulates his imagination, senses new possibilities about the condition of being alive. If an esthetic moment which may otherwise occur by chance is to be considered as an art experience, it must include an object made for the purpose of that experience by a creator, or creators, and a viewer who can respond to that object or objects. It is also important to understand that the viewer must, in fact, respond to the art object, not merely see it.

From here we will examine, in order, the three terms of the art experience and the esthetic moment it embodies from a theoretical model constructed to illuminate it. The trouble with models is that they are taken literally; they become more important than the ideas they illustrate and take on a life of their own which has a tendency to reduce the original conceptions to an absurdity. This tendency is one we shall have to admit from the outset. We will keep in mind that the various abstractions we are about to examine are, after all, merely abstractions, not the thing itself. The thing itself is the esthetic moment caused through an art experience. It is ineffable. We are forced to get as close as words and models will permit while remembering *it* will not appear; that *it* is a thing we are only talking about, that the systematic description of its elements is a word trick which will bring us to, but not inside, the art experience. Just as scenery for a play, the models have a limited use.

If the ability of an object to stimulate the esthetic moment depends upon the participation of an unknown viewer, can we talk about an object being more or less successful as the result of the skill of the creator? Are there guidelines for the making of an object which a teacher can pass on to the student? There are, if we agree to recognize creators as their own viewer; if we admit that they judge their work with the awareness that it must interest and stimulate others. As they build, artists take two roles; maker and viewer. They are critical, moved or unmoved, by their own work. They intelligently construct it to say "a thing" even though they might not be able to translate what they say in words or any other medium, even though an observer might find their process of work hectic and seemingly haphazard. Obviously, it is a "saying" which would be complete within its own expressive possibility. If so, sound, formal symbols, smells and taste would only detract from it instead of enhancing or explaining it. The work of art explains itself, or fails to be a work of art. If it needs outside help, it becomes merely a one way story from the object to a viewer, who may listen to or even assent to, but not participate in its discourse.

There are a variety of approaches and tastes, a variety of theories of design and feelings which the artists respond to as they build. But this should not prevent us from drawing general principles and describing the requirements for making an object **which could lead to** an art experience. In other words, we will examine the rules for making objects, with confidence in the position that such rules exist and can be demonstrated and taught by artists to pupils. We may not know who will be moved to experience and esthetic moment by an object, but **we can propose general conditions for making, which will make that occurrence more likely**.

As we discuss creators and their task, we will also take up the character of the object and develop an understanding of the viewer's role in the esthetic moment.

Consideration of the work of creators immediately opens a whole series of topics. Artists deal with materials and content. They exert technique to manipulate them, and so become aware of form. Surely no word has meant so much or so little as form when we use it to describe the unity and the essence of an object which leads us to an art experience. In this discussion, form will be restricted to the domain of the viewer. **When the viewer is led to perceive the unity or essence of the object and possesses the esthetic moment, we will assume the object has final form**. Final form is an attribute which the viewer ascribes to the object, not an attribute inherent in the object. This does not mean we can dismiss it from our attention any more than the artist can dismiss the viewer from his or her attention. It remains important for we choose to use it as a description of a successful art object; an object which has given rise to an esthetic moment. The word form as it is used to describe a particular set of formal conditions or the total area of one medium used in art, poses no problem. We are concerned here only with its use as a description for the essence or unity or final condition of the object. In that sense, the word has little meaning by itself to the artist. The artist is concerned with more specific terms. Form is a critic's word and should be assigned by viewers, and artists acting as their own viewer, who will have arrived at their own refinement, or confusion, of its meaning.

The creator's task, regardless of their medium, is clearly defined. They must abstract from their material those elements which they can manipulate to carry forward and illuminate their content. They are concerned, then, with as many specifics as they are able to distinguish and use. These are the design elements.

These elements vary with the materials used and they even vary with the ability of the artist to perceive and make use of them. Artists are aware of form just as they are aware of a viewer. As the artist works, he or she is both a viewer and an artist, but the artist's awareness is more precise. He or she is concerned with all of the specifics; design elements, which will make up the total effect or design composition of the object. Most of all, the artist is conscious of manipulation or technique. The artist's action with the elements he or she comprehends must have a rationale. It may involve a total response based on momentary body feel, or it may be a strategy of carefully controlled sequences. But each of these, and any other less extreme approach to work, embodies a content and a direction; an idea and a technique. The work of the artist may be conceived as:

$$\frac{(technique)\ (content)}{(material)} = art\ object$$

The decision to place technique and content as the terms of a numerator is based simply on the conviction that those are the most important aspects of the creator's task and that materials not properly chosen or controlled have a tendency to overwhelm and reduce technique and content. We might even suppose that when an art object is granted final form by a viewer that the terms achieve unity or one. But we must quickly remind ourselves that the unity exists in the art object only for *that* viewer; the viewer who experiences an esthetic moment from it. Others might view the object as out of balance, uninteresting, and not capable of drawing their participation.

The decision to place technique first stems from two sources. It is the single most important element in the work of art. Good ideas and good materials are useless without it; they become merely intentions or pretentions. It is the shaper and catalyst of the art experience. If technique fails all is lost; if it succeeds we are moved, even by second rate materials and common ideas. Also technique is, far and away, the most complex aspect of making that an artist faces.

Technique is manipulation. It is the force we bring to bear on design elements in order to direct our materials to focus on the content we have in mind. Materials express and illuminate the content. Design elements are the abstractions we have in mind while manipulating the material. They are the unity we work with; textures, words, colors, beats, measures, steps, scenes, chapters, tones, and other things, depending on the medium we use. They are fairly evident and we are used to thinking in their terms. But identifying them and using them are two separate considerations. The first is quite simple when compared with the second.

What is the force that so directs manipulation that it communicates to others? Certainly we cannot fully describe it for we do not fully know it. It is the essence of technique and would extend to every limit to which a single successful effort had pushed it. It is a process in which artists are able to keep in mind the needs of their content, their material, and their viewer. It is the point of decision which selects the tool, plans the stroke, and asks if the idea has been carried or aborted. It is continuous, logical, intuitive, historical and projective. Above all, it is communication, not in an ordinary sense of merely making information common, but in an extraordinary sense which will carry emotion; the quality and attitude of a point of view, the feelings of one person or group of persons expressed to others. The communication must be so apt and precise that it will invite the participation of another and let them, in partnership with it, discover new possibilities about the condition of being alive, not only once, but perhaps over and over again.

The requirements are so staggering it is a wonder anyone seriously proposes to make art the work of his life. But like all adventures, the unlikely success is filled with such fine opportunities artists sweep failures aside and continue relentlessly on. Art is a humane endeavor. When a person is able to express the deepest feelings he or she possesses to another person they form the strongest bond human experience has been able to discover. That bond is found when the esthetic moment makes available the *emotional* sympathy and compassion which the feelings of one of us fully revealed to another will inspire. In this regard art experience has no rivals and no substitutes. Its power of communication shapes men and creates the best circumstances for maintaining and appreciating life that humanity has been able to achieve.

If an esthetic moment carries a good deal more than mere information, the artist must be able, through his or her technique, to reach and stimulate the viewer's imagination. If that communication takes place there must be a single element or set of elements which we assume can stir up feelings in others which would otherwise remain inaccessible.

At this point, recognizing that an art object stimulates many levels of communication, we will restrict the discussion of technique and communication to just one of these: the sensual communication. We will assume that it offers nearest entry to the wordless, intuitive, physical responses which are the earliest, strongest, and most persistent sensations of being alive we possess.

When Goethe, in his *Maxims and Reflections*, states "There is something magical in rhythm; it even makes us believe that the sublime lies within our reach," he reminds us of a single element which artists and philosophers have felt compelled to come with, each in their own way again and again. Rhythm appeals directly to our sensual, physical awareness. It expresses many phenomena with which we are surrounded: night and day, hot and cold, up and down, sun and moon, advance, and retreat, expand and contract, walking running, tides, hammering, wind waves, songs, rapids, flying birds, mountains, clouds, talk – all of which set up a sense of rightness and appropriateness for rhythm. Everywhere we see, hear, and feel a thing – an interval – a thing – an interval – a thing to keep us keenly aware of life's sequences and changes. Rhythm is woven into our lives. It speaks to us directly. It will carry us off against our will when we are engaged in something else. It compels us to respond. It puts idiotic phrases and snatches of music we dislike in our head and forces them into our consciousness again and again at inappropriate times. Hunger and satisfaction, asleep and awake, in motion and still – our whole lives are lived in a constant rhythm of muscular tension and relaxations. There is no way for us to consciously escape rhythmic patterns. Our blood, our breath, and our very lives depend upon it.

Rhythm represents even more than this. It suggests the profound cosmic pattern of order and chaos. It carries the dark truth we sense; the one which we create religions to protect us from. We live in an indifferent environment. If passion and arrogance sweep us to disaster is it because we pressed the order we depended upon beyond its outer limit and came into a larger realm of probability where chance must serve us with chaos. Our society and our own lives are lives in a constant rhythm of order and chaos. When we restore equilibrium in one area, change causes a new crisis in another. We are forever off balance, but seek to restore it so we may proceed with our lives in an orderly fashion – anticipating, correcting, and adjusting events we are familiar with. But so many forces are at work and conditions change so fast we are always put in the position of catching up once more. We are in a state of constant conflict where we pit our ability to order and stabilize our lives against the larger condition of chance or chaos.

Rhythm itself is chaos and order. It repeats and varies, repeats and varies. Repetition calls our attention to order, variation causes us to be aware of change. To perceive any pattern, the first requirement is repetition. Communication depends upon it. But sensual communication, which is to reach deeper and carry more, must establish fidelity to our living condition. To render repetition as valid, worthy of belief, and relevant to experience, variation is required. Never quite at rest, never at completion or fulfillment, repetition and variation set up a rhythm of change which we intuitively grasp as *most true.* Death is a completion, a concept of unchanging, timeless nothing. Its opposite is life. There is no way to talk about life without recognizing recurrence and similarity which repetition abstracts from experience. Its necessary counterpart of change, direction and chance, is abstracted through variation. The play of imbalance between repetition and variation sets up the rhythm we sense to be most true, most believable, most real. Rhythm is a sensation which universally establishes an awareness of existence. It is immediate, and powerful. It is the indispensable force of manipulation which the artist exerts on materials and content in order to permit final form to be achieved. All phases of technique must be put to the service of rhythm. By itself rhythm is an art form. Its own possibilities are great even before we borrow its powers for a specific medium. Without conscious use of its ability to take possession of us, the artist could not create an object which would provide access to the esthetic moment.

There is another facet of rhythm which we must clearly understand if we are to appreciate the integrity of its meaning. C.H. Waddington, in a chapter of L.L. Whyte's *Aspect of Form*, indicates that in the organic state, form may be said to be in equilibrium, but not in perfect balance since organic form is ever subject to changes in development. There is order but it is incomplete; not totally resolved. Instead it may be said to be potentially resolved. This conception intuitively corresponds with our larger awareness of the balance between order and chaos. So too, with art experience. To totally resolve a complicated statement reflecting the human condition is patently impossible. Art objects are subject to, and must appeal to, esthetic responses which lie deep enough to require absolute fidelity to the living condition. Non-living art, or pat solutions to complicated sets of circumstances are dehumanized artistic failures, which, at best, may intelligently construct a logical discourse, but that is all. This is not to say that artists must attempt to duplicate the multiple forces of nature's organic form. But fidelity to the unresolved rhythm of order-change-chaos and order is essential to every object of art.

This has a direct and specific implication for the artist's work as it applies to technique. The viewer may ascribe final form, which is only another way of saying he experiences the esthetic moment, but an artist cannot carry the object to a point of final solution. The only true finality we anticipate and respond to, is death. The goal of total completion contains two serious faults. First, the condition of life which provides the context for the artist, the object, and the viewer is defied or made false. The object becomes pretty, sentimental, or pretentious. Second, the viewer is excluded from participation. The object commands and the viewer obeys. Artists, in their making, and the object, as their product, are filled with contempt. There is no room for the imagination of another. We sense the assumption that the viewer's investment is unworthy. In their making, artists must appreciate both the commitment of a viewer and their own responsibility to react to the conditions of life as it is. Total resolution or final completion will render the work as exclusive and lifeless. It will become a declaration instead of an invitation. That is to say, it will be unlikely to permit any stronger emotion than mere admiration.

At this point two cautions are in order. We recognize that chance esthetic moments occur and that viewer's predispositions, talents, and experiences vary widely. Therefore, we must never exclude the possibility of any art object's giving rise to an esthetic moment and earning the attributes we have called final form. But, as pointed out earlier, intelligent making, based on an understanding of what art is and what it involves, is necessarily aware of requirements which will be more likely to encourage the esthetic moment to take place. The whole study and development of technique rests upon that assumption.

Next, we must add that the notion of simply leaving a work unfinished, or its content not completely felt or thought, with the expectation that any agile viewer will be likely to furnish missing parts and gain an art experience is false. Artists must do his their work and viewers theirs. Their roles are not the same with respect to the art object. And their relationship is not such that artists can conceive of themselves as running ninety yards of a one hundred yard dash, confident that some viewer will come by happy to run the last ten. The statement, i.e., the object, whether it be a sculpture, play or dance, must be completed, finished, resolved, by the only one capable of doing it: the creator, the professional, the artist, who knows the work and the intention for it and appreciates the requirement of an investment from a viewer. But within the object is embedded an unresolved rhythm. It both reflects the condition of constant imbalance between order and chaos and serves as an invitation for viewers to become involved, re-experience the living condition on new terms, and discover new possibilities about it and themselves.

Viewers may or may not create personal resolutions for themselves as they confront the object. That specific response is not necessary. But the work must make room for them, not by the absence of technique and content, but by the presence of these. In fact, the work itself must be consummated so well that the viewer can readily perceive its range and mood and be drawn by its specifics to arrange themselves in it and discover the object's possibilities. In other words, the statement is complete, but *must always be an understatement*. It must excite the viewer's imagination, not command, overwhelm, or cudgel them. It is a subtle thing. One stroke, one short paragraph, one gesture, can turn the corner, and an otherwise successful understatement becomes propaganda or a grandiose resolution relevant to nothing we care about.

Before we leave the topic of rhythm, one more point should be brought to light. Rhythm permits the fusion of the general with the specific. Its own reference is broad and impersonal. It allows us a remove and heightens our perspective. Rhythm, by itself, embodies an esthetic distance. Its own scope which refers to so much, in and around us, keeps us aware of universal and omnipresent sensations of experience. This characteristic of rhythm makes it an ideal vehicle for the specific. A particular case is brought into perspective, its focus is made more intense, its joy and poignancy expanded, its tragedy made serene, by the larger reference rhythm implies.

In his book *The Meaning of Art*, Herbert Read tells us: "In a perfect work of art all the elements are interrelated; they cohere to form a unity which has a value greater than the mere sum of these elements."

Perhaps the perfect work of art does not exist, but Read's analysis of the compliance, interlocking, and balance of elements offers a full appreciation of the complexity and possibility of design.

So far, in our discussion of technique, we have concentrated on rhythm; analyzed its powers and pointed out its final importance. As part of that development we mentioned design elements and characterized these as being the smallest understandable units with which the artist works. We spoke of technique's being the spirit and force which manipulated these design elements. At this point, another diagram may make the meaning clearer.
The original formulation of:

$$\frac{(technique)\ (content)}{(material)} = art\ object$$

can be expanded slightly and rendered in this manner:

$$technique = (rhythm\ of\ repetition\ \&\ variation)\ of\ (design\ elements)$$

As we recognized, design elements depend upon the medium selected for the content's expression. One example might be a single color woodcut. In that instance the generic formulation which is now

$$\frac{(rhythm\ of\ repeats\ \&\ variations)(design\ elements)(content)}{(material)} = art\ object$$

would become:

$$\frac{(rhythm\ of\ repeats/\ variations)(lines/tones/textures/spaces)(content)}{(material)} = art\ object$$

Another example might be an oil painting described this way:

$$\frac{(rhythm\ of\ repeats/variation)(line/tone/texture/space/color)(content)}{(material)} = art\ object$$

Or a stone sculpture:

$$\frac{(rhythm\ of\ repeats/\ variations)(light/textures/outlines/mass)(content)}{(material)} = art\ object$$

    There is a temptation to go on and on playing word games. Perhaps all that would be accomplished would be a clear demonstration of how different artists seize upon different sets of design elements. By choosing a mathematical type of model, we cannot hope to borrow an equivalent sense of certainty. The above formulations are used only to suggest relationships, and define elements which are the aspects of creating we must consider if we are to better comprehend the role of the creator as it applies to the esthetic moment.

    One more term will be useful to us: design composition. It refers to the total effect of the artist. It is the product of manipulation of design elements. It refers to the final state of the object as it leaves the artist's hand and before it is subject to the response of the viewer. Going back to the generic formulation, we would find design composition use as follows:

$$\frac{(technique)\ (content)}{(material)} = art\ object$$

  The phrase is reasonably descriptive and will help to distinguish the product from the process when we use the word design. Design composition is the concluding arrangement of design elements into the pattern of the final product. Presumably, it embeds a content into a rhythm of repetition and variation which expresses the order-change-chaos-order progression of life. The design composition may be nearly balanced and serene, or disjointed and hectic. It must convey the organization, restraint, cohesiveness and order of repetition on one hand and the newness, excitement, and freedom of variation on the other; and in such balance the mood and intent carry all that is meant of the content and nothing which is not meant, and all that in such a manner that the design composition, or object, is sufficiently understated to invite a viewer's esthetic moment.

  Are there exceptions to the imbalance of rhythm? We think of sun symbols in sculpture and painting, or religious insignia. The design composition there is a conclusive monad, free from variation and in perfect balance. Do they inspire esthetic moments and earn the attribute of final form? The baffling answer seems to be 'yes'. But the nature of these creations suggests other influences of predisposition and belief which may either override the esthetic moment altogether, substituting something else for it, or which may bolster and enhance it because these symbols have such a special and unique meaning. Exceptions exist and should be noted.

  We began this section by outlining what was meant by the art experience and identified the three major necessary elements of it. Choosing to discuss the first of these, we concerned ourselves with the creator. All of the previous examination has focused on one part of the creator's work: technique. Two other aspects of the artist's job of making are content and materials. Materials are self-evident for the purposes of this discussion, so we will pass on to content, about which, some comments are in order.

  Content is what artists 'say'. It reveals their mood and attitude. It exposes their feelings to others openly and clearly. It is the total response they makes to their own subject and matter, distilled to remove the flotsam and jetsam of random emotional paraphernalia. All of their knowledge and feeling are committed to the purpose of making their statement clear. They do not consciously hold back, but instead are compelled to express all. Content quickly reveals their sensual intelligence, the limits of their awareness, and the special interests they entertain. Content sets a limit above which no amount of technique can carry it. It is a window in upon humankind's sensibility and as we will see, it is the most important factor in determining whether the object is vulgar or rare. It is an artist's personal statement, whether he or she paints landscapes or inscapes, vilifies or praises their subject. In each case it is an intent which technique must match and carry forward skillfully. Clearly, some statements are simpler and easier than others and some formal arrangements which fix and restrict the boundaries of the effort are easier to use than others. Content and technique must meet in an appropriate setting, one where both will be permitted the greatest freedom to exercise their powers – together. Is the content better expressed in stone or a lyric poem? If stone, what size, what kind, color, and texture; what scale? Would a song express the content better? And so on. These are the considerations all artists must make. Often they will conclude the exact flavor of the content requires a formal arrangement or medium beyond their range of skills. The ideas must change or be temporarily abandoned. In general, content dictates the formal arrangement and the medium and artist chooses.

   The notion that we can choose between ideas and technique and elevate one above the other is a remainder of the worst which an academic approach to art has left us. To permit achievement of an art experience, an object must have technique. Earlier the view was expressed that good technique can carry vulgar content and materials to an esthetic moment. Vulgar or common content is capable of being incorporated into an art experience, but bad technique is not. There is no hierarchy of technique. Either it carries the content or it utterly fails. It will vary from artist to artist and appeal to one viewer and not another. But the technique must be sufficiently skillful to move the viewer, or the object has no relationship to art experience.

   Is there any sensible way of speaking of degrees of skill in technique above and beyond a minimum of carrying the content to an esthetic moment? There would be, if we are also willing to admit degrees of esthetic response. If one art experience is somehow greater than another, it seems likely that both content and technique play a part in that hierarchy of intensity. From our own experience and that of others, we know such a hierarchy does, indeed, exist and that esthetic moments are not equivalent either in quality or in power. We can, in other words, admit degrees of intensity in technique, but only beyond that point where an esthetic moment is made possible by the object for at least one viewer. The point is that content has a much wider latitude. There are many entrances for content to be welcomed into mind and many levels of interest and commitment to entertain it, but technique must pass through only one: the sensual-physical spectrum of response. It is precise and demanding. Either its standard of utter fidelity to the larger condition of life awareness is met, or entry fails.

But pure technique is as irrelevant and helpless without content as content, regardless of its high purpose, is without technique. The argument of realists for technique as opposed to the arguments of non-objectivists for content only signifies how crippled we now are when we cope with art experience. Art experience is open, gracious, and filled with possibility.

In this section we have taken up the subject of art experience and the conditions under which it comes about. In particular, we have focused upon the creators and their work. In the course of that discussion we have suggested a formulation of their task which separately considers technique, content, and material, and introduced the concepts of design elements, design composition, and final form. We have refereed to, and described, the art object as we analyzed the artist's work, and we have made some preliminary inferences about the viewer. At this point, we will examine in more detail the viewer's role in the esthetic moment art experience offers, and once more, we shall turn attention upon the object – about which, both the creator and viewer are concerned.

It is not accurate to speak of art as a universal language. The key force of technique, rhythm, repetitions, and variations is universal and design elements are often, but not always, universally understood. But the design composition tends only to be effective as an elicitor of esthetic moments within broad cultural and/or regional limitations. Too many factors and too much historical vision and prejudice are incorporated in the final product to render it accessible to all. Too much variation between people exists for us to depend upon any single object's earning the accolade of final form from everyone, even within one segment of one culture. Too much change in our heritage, values, and disposition occurs over time to expect an object to readily stimulate viewers for all time to come. Art objects do not speak to everyone and they do not speak deathless prose or otherwise communicate for eternity. They are, like their creators and viewers, mortal. We have no evidence that they enjoy special privilege when it comes to extinction. The hazards of neglect, war, new directions, and other natural disasters are bound to overtake all of them.

If art is understood to be an experience in the communication of intuitively felt and rationally comprehended insight and possibility about the condition of existence, and if that awareness is discovered through the viewer's own participation in the esthetic moment, the scope and limits of making and responding to art is very broad. We must be prepared to admit three distinct levels of influence which will encourage or discourage the esthetic moment as it occurs between a particular object and a particular viewer.

The first of these are contemporaneous cultural differences. The ragas of India, a Navajo corn dance, *Death of a Salesman*, Japanese No drama, and Wagnerian opera are culturally embedded. They draw much of their strength from this condition and would, very likely, be meaningless to vast numbers of people from other cultures for whom art experience normally plays an important life role. For most, the esthetic moment would be lost.

A second level is found within a given culture. Here we see the great range of differences which separate viewers by virtue of their capacity, training, and experience. Once we admit the viewer as participant, we have to admit as many possibilities for art experience as there are viewers to sense it. An experience of being confronted by an object which leaves one individual unmoved does not permit that person to conclude the object is not art or not capable of moving another to an esthetic appreciation. The fact is, that it is not *his or her* art; it may be too common or too rare an object, but whether one prefers it or not, it still may fulfill all the requirements of the art experience for others. Everywhere people are endeavoring to build objects which have only the function of providing art experience. Their efforts may command large or small audiences or no audience at all. Art is not served by makers and viewers divided into separate sets of audiences and regarding one another with contempt. The contemptuous manner in which the phrase 'non-art' is used to describe another's result or a viewer's response serves only to demonstrate how seriously the effect of a divided mind and a cramped sensibility prevents us from understanding what art is and what it involves. Members of the same culture living in the same span of time will, and should differ widely over what they choose for esthetic moments. Why should they react otherwise since they are responding to separate histories, separate sets of bone and muscle and nerve, and separate awareness of their own needs and expectations?

   Last, we have differences on the level of time. Art as an endeavor and an experience may be immortal. For, as we know, new ideas and objects are brought forth in affirmation and rebuttal. But individual objects and single ideas or systems are extinguished in the process of new rounds toward a large appreciation of life's mystery. Only the spirit and direction remain. Art objects mean many things. Among these, they serve, in part, as an intensified reflection of their age's commitments and values. There may be master works so conceived that they could stand for eternity, but they will not be given that possibility since they are physical objects and are subject to inevitable destruction. At another extreme are objects which refer so precisely to the unique characteristics of their time that they cannot survive the imminent change which will sweep away the immediate conditions they refer to. We recognize that some art forms are more vulnerable to change than others. We also see most art objects which succeed in providing art experience will pale to subsequent viewers given enough time to permit change in values and life style. Even our master works, if they could be viewed in a millennium to come, would very likely be looked upon a curiosities and antiques rather than catalysts for an esthetic moment.

   The viewer represents both the possibility for, and limits of, the art experience. There are no images one can rely upon when using the phrase "good taste" or "bad taste", except personal ones. We hear people say "that is art", or "that is not art", on the basis of whatever capacity and experience has created their own image of what good and bad taste are. The act of judgment which decides whether an art experience is possible, or not, has its own internal validity, but we must understand that it remains individual and subjective.

Whatever one chooses to serve as an object leading to art experience is a valid art object as long as two conditions are met. First, the object must have been made with the intention of providing art experience. If not, the esthetic moment was encountered in it by chance. That moment may be equally profound and moving, but since it is felt under any set of random or imposed conditions, without a creator's intent to communicate through his art, it would seem inappropriate to label it as an art experience. Second, the object so intended must provide the viewer with the esthetic moment the experience of art offers.

A host of problems arise at this point. With such a broad definition, or a narrow definition with such broad implications, or art, are there no standards, no levels of taste, nor objective measures upon which we may scale the scope and penetration of various objects of art? The
Answer clearly is, no. There must be objectively shaped criticism and analysis of works of art. These serve to feed, stimulate, and expand the reach of both artists and viewers. The work of the critic is indispensable to the appreciation of art experience's possibility. But no matter how objective the analysis or precise the standards may be, they are valid only as a viewpoint, only as a way of talking about art work. The critic's effort ultimately may serve to open, or to close avenues for experience enjoyed by others, but it will not alter the fundamental elements and requirements of the esthetic moment.

Criticism is always valid and necessary. The difficulty with criticism in art today is that critics have almost no one to speak with. They carry their discourse back and forth between themselves and the few artists who are sufficiently wise or insufficiently courageous to be aware of what critics need to say. There is no robust community or interested parties to take issue or elaborate on their work. Their quarrels become family affairs and include some distasteful aspects of that relationship. In short, they are neglected because they are discussing an area which is actively submerged in public and private life. Nothing seems more irrelevant to the flow of life today than art or anyone who proposes to seriously discuss it. The artist and art critic share the effects of mutual distrust in which sensual-physical intuitive responses are held. It is quite natural, when our audience becomes smaller and smaller, to want to do something about it. Usually we take on a forceful approach. We begin to command or even shout. We hope, somehow, to straighten people up and demonstrate by our own intensity what they are missing. But the overwhelming weight of public disposition is to ignore the critic and the artist. No amount of conviction on the part of critics, or loud demonstrations from the stage, canvas or novel will alter the desperate condition of this imbalance. It will be a long struggle which must be conducted with patience, even when our blindness aims us directly toward destruction. We need more criticism and more people to care about it. Criticism about art is not art experience. It runs parallel to that experience and its whole intention is to support it.

Is there a real difference between fine arts and crafts? This distinction, like others, is a construct which has proved useful in certain situations in the past. But it implies divisions within art experience which do not exist and leads us to approach the objects these categories include from a restricted point of view. The word "fine", as applied to art, conveys an impression that some art is finished, excellent, and distilled pure as compared with art which is not. But custom has so enlarged this tattered word that it means other things; one form of art as over against another. Surely its usefulness is ended when it divides the experience one finds in all jewelry and all drama from that found in all sculpture and all painting. Ceramics and architecture enjoy a half-life in fine arts confines depending upon the predilections of the moment and the individual. Perhaps the art experience of music is quite different from that of drawing, but all art experiences are distinct regardless of the form and the medium giving rise to them. The bad effect is one of creating a false division. It is worsened by adding a prejudice of excellence and superiority on one hand and disparagement on the other.

"Folk art" is another questionable term. Bill Broonzy, when invited by Studs Terkal to make a comment on the distinction between folk music and blues, replied that as far as he knew, there were just blues and it took folks to sing all of them. The observation could not have been made better. For all art experiences we need creators, and viewers. There seems to be no advantage gained by dividing either into categories of "folk" and who knows what.

There is a distinction which can be useful that is current today. It is particularly pertinent because it carries the sense of a difference in commitment between the word and the phrase: entertainment and art experience. These are two separate experiences even when found in different parts of the same work. Musical plays, as we have created them in the United States, are primarily entertaining. That is, they hold our attention, divert, and amuse us. Generally they do not stimulate deeper responses, but on occasion they do. We are moved to discover, here and there, the full lift and enlightenment of an esthetic moment. We are transported, made aware of new perspectives and new possibilities. Are we to characterize the total work as art, or entertainment? Perhaps a simple category would not be possible. Instead of comforting ourselves with one conception, perhaps we should hold two in our minds when we think of that work.

Usually this distinction is fairly clear, and for us, at present, it is very important. Singers, comics, revues, bands, jugglers, adventure stories and sports events do not require the same commitment or provide the same expectations as the esthetic moment art can provide. We "pass the time" with them or "take the pressure off". Our powers of belief are relaxed. We want time to pass pleasantly and wish to live without reference to our convictions and problems. We drift, talk, think of other things in a casual chain of states of awareness. It is enough and we are satisfied. We are diverted and amused.

The viewer can be taken by surprise. Chance esthetic moments seem often to catch us unready. But in an instant we are involved and sensing all of it. Art experiences also possess us the same way. But we are usually prepared. We have consciously put ourselves in the way of objects and hope to acquire all the experience can provide. We make ready in other ways. We study, look, talk, touch, listen, again and again swinging wider circles each time to enrich our precious moments and make way for fresh responses. We actively participate from the start. We trouble ourselves to become knowledgeable. Entertainment, on the other hand, is a passive event. It is neither stiff nor demanding in any sense. All that is necessary is to cut adrift from our cares and shift our attention.

R.P. Blackmur, speaking on the topic of *A Burden for Critics* for the 1948 Bollingen Lecture Series, states: "The audience is able to bring less to the work of art than under conditions of the old culture, and the artist is required to bring more. What has changes its aspect is the way the institutions, the conceptions, the experience of culture gets into the arts. What has happened is what was said above; almost the whole job of culture has been dumped on the artists' hands."

All we need add to this statement is to note the clear affirmation of Blackmur's point provided by popular culture in overwhelming amounts. The audience brings less to art experience and the audience is diminished despite the massive doses of exposure and training required in public schools.

This development of the elements of art has opened consideration of the art experience to include all esthetic moments provided by objects constructed for that purpose. The experience of art exists on many levels of culture, experience, and capacity. It ranges from common to rare works of art.

We took the position that a design composition guided by general principles, which included awareness of the crucial power of rhythm, design elements, content, and appropriate selection of material, or form and medium, would be more likely to communicate and encourage the esthetic moment to take place. We recognized three levels of influence which tend to shift and replace the excitement and fidelity of old art objects with new ones: inter-cultural influences, intra-cultural influences, and cultural influences as they are subject to change over time. We spoke of the viewer's participation as active and mentioned the necessity for the creator's technique to understate the content and so leave room for the viewer's involvement. We pointed out the problem which the divided mind creates for art experience in our time.

We will now rearrange the original formulation to include the attribute of final form, make some comments about that conception, and move on to new considerations. The concluding formulation is:

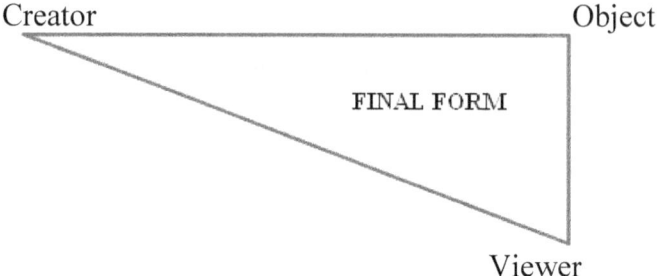

The concept *final form* refers simply to the state of an art object which has given rise to the esthetic moment in at least one viewer. We have described the esthetic moment realizing that such a description was at a remove from experiencing it, and concluded that unless the technique of the artist was sure, it could not take place. Final form represents the investment of the viewer, as well as the investment of the artist, in the object which inspires it. While the object is complete from the artist's hand, its content is understated. In this sense, the viewer's participation represents his or her own conclusion of the object's communication.

ART AND SOCIETY

Art experience provides esthetic moments. It occurs when an object appeals to the total mind: perception, intuition, and logic. We respond to it intellectually and emotionally. But we live in a time when mind seems to be divided and the total response which art experience requires is less likely to be encouraged than at any time in the past.

In the forward to his book *Vision in Motion*, Moholy-Nagy speaks of the necessity of relating mind and body forces to attain, what might be termed, a full spectrum experience. No doubt, he is thoroughly aware of the dangers of this simple dualism. Mind itself, may or may not have a number of different functions and divisions, but if it has, surely there are many and form a coalition of multiple processes which are essentially cooperative in nature. But when we encounter conditions for mental process as if simple division were actually the case, we must either talk directly to that division, or avoid coping with its effects altogether. Let us affirm that we understand the human mind is too complex for us to comprehend in the illogical terms with which we are now familiar. Until we discover conclusive evidence to the contrary, we may rest assured that mental process does not exist in a simple relationship of opposing halves.

In this section, just as in the last and those to come, we will refer to sensual-physical and intuitive sources of response on one hand, and logical-rational and objective sources of response on the other. It is understood that these are descriptions of two phases of mental activity which historical prejudice forces us to respond to. It is also understood that these do *not* oppose one another in any way, despite what we have learned about that opposition from moral teachings and the startling thrust of public mood for objectified experience. When we pose intuition and subjectivity versus rationality and objectivity as if they were in conflict, we recognize only the existence of a past prejudice and current public faith, not the actual condition of mental process.

This division is omnipresent. We will have occasion to turn to it again and again and force back upon ourselves the discomfort of that well disguised and thoroughly entrenched point of view: man has two parts to his soul, two to his heart, and two to his mind. To destroy this myth of opposing twos, the invidious counterplay in the decisions of nearly every back woodsman and chairman of the board, we must expose it wherever it abides. It is the enemy of the esthetic moment. We cannot appreciate the meaning and possibility of art experience without constant reference to its damaging influence.

Previously we spoke of art as an institution in contrast with the view that art is an experience. We will now examine the difference between these and analyze the demands they make on society.

Art, like other experiences, has tended to become impersonal and objective. The prevalent view is that we ought to seek truth through science and beauty through art. This leaves a number of things unsettled. First, art is no closer to beauty than science. The marvelous formulations of relationships found in the latter are inspiring, universal, and austere. One can gawk at the formulas and explanations with unbridled admiration for their serenity and symmetry. They are beautiful, too, but often they are only provocative and discomforting. Occasionally they are ugly and even frightening.

Second, science is no closer to truth than art. It is infinitely more powerful in the physical world and provides the only dependable means we have of manipulating that world. But our sense of world extends way beyond mere manipulation. We are first aware of existence in general, and our own being in particular, as marvelous mysteries. Our response to our own physical and psychic world is the single most important source of information with which we must deal. It is not subject to objective determinations except on the most minimal and superficial terms. If all the expectations we hold for science are realize, this will still remain true. There is, then, a subjective truth which is, at least, as important as fluoride in drinking water, polio vaccine, and information about nuclear reaction. It arrives in many ways and on many levels, but it is sensed most urgently in the esthetic moment. Since art experience is an esthetic moment we actively contrive, we must hold that art experience is also a source of knowledge and a seeking of truth.

But the popular proposition that we seek truth through science and beauty through art does not admit that what art seeks is also knowledge and truth. It takes the position that subjective truth is personal, trivial, even selfish, hence unworthy of serious examination. We are taught to submerge our feelings – our personal responses – and to submit our conscious lives to the objective light that others demand in order to understand us. *We do not recognize that others would also understand our subjective responses.* We realize that they "learn" and we have "learned", that all we need are the facts we can agree on, and all else is too dark, too tangled, and too passionate and sinful for us to cope with. There is but one fate for art experience: define it, locate it, and limit it. Art is to have a separate life. We are to cage it as one would a boa constrictor; put it in a distinct place where one can move out of life's normal routines to view it in limited context, then disengage and return to real life clean, uncontaminated, and in possession of new facts put on the card next to its cage. The effort to limit and control art and to appreciate it as a sociological phenomenon rather than a direct subject experience has succeeded. We have removed art experience as a regular recurrent activity from our lives. In its place we have substituted the esthetic moment encountered by chance, and entertainment. These make no demands and leave us free to pursue, objectively, the details of existence and the larger truths which common practice and science respectively reveal.

This work has required some doing. But, the ingenuity and relentless purpose of zealots is great, and in this matter, the zealots have been many and their influence prolonged and powerful. Art has been institutionalized. It is encouraged in limited amounts under certain conditions with specific and **objective** purposes in view. We are to learn about it as one learns about any intellectual endeavor. We study its history, its great men, its high points of achievement; we de develop systems and schools and periods to organize our facts; we propose criteria to help us distinguish the false from the true, the good from the bad. We set up institutions to house it, institutions to encourage it, institutions to study it, institutions to sell it, and institutions to judge it. We say that art is valuable and must be kept alive. We call upon civic clubs, municipal committees, wealthy patrons, foundations, and the government to protect and nurture it. We form vast armies of officials to manage the effort. They merge into the larger community and require the services of administrators, janitors, accountants, guards, sales people, technology, machinery, documentation, publicity people, fundraisers, builders, and the like.

What has happened to the art experience itself? Exactly what was intended. It remains outside, and incidental to, art as a business, art as an institution. It is kept within strict limits and contexts which are considered appropriate and approved exceptions to the general flow of life. The experience is surrounded by experts who are prepared to save people from themselves. They translate, arbitrate, abstract, and distill art experience into pamphlets, articles, and books of information. We know more about art, but we feel less about it.

The influences and single acts which brought this condition into existence, was, of course, not a conscious conspiracy to defame and minimize art. Its intention was to protect art. But it came about under highly unfavorable prejudices and was founded upon assumptions which were not cognizant of the fact that art is an experience, not an object, and that passion and intuition are not inherently evil. Under the circumstances we might be amazed that art has been permitted even a separate life. Perhaps, we ought to be grateful that we have the institution and business of art to put objects into focus at all. At least artists are at work, a few viewers know their contribution, and critics have something real to respond to. But what little sense of obligation and respect that we feel toward those who saw *something* worthy in art must not deter us from pointing out the serious defects in the institutional structure.

As an institution and a business, art has given rise to a new breed of art people. They are not primarily involved with art as a catalyst for esthetic moments. They came to it for other reasons: direct profits, therapy, prestige, amusement, and investments. They make objects, buy and sell objects, live with objects, and talk about objects for one or another of the reasons mentioned. They are important. To the general public, they represent a knowledgeable group of skilled amateurs and professionals. Their opinions are valued, particularly when they acquire the status of experts, which institutions and officialdom inevitably create. They surround the various separate institutions and serve as go-betweens in that space which separates the institution itself from the public at large.

The art functionary becomes an arbiter of elegance. Their opinions tend to go unchallenged, for they do not speak to a broad, responsive public which is familiar with art experience. Their public is passive, and if they listen at all, they have usually agreed tacitly and unconsciously in advance to accept the expert's word as the final guide for their own judgment. In other words, we create experts on the assumption that a knowing about art is the necessary and sufficient criteria to select them, and turn them loose on a public which is unfamiliar with esthetic decisions. Other than vague rumblings and complaints from artists who instinctively turn away from such elaborate games, there exists a vast and unbroken silence. Any opinion will do as long as an expert is speaking.

Joseph Wood Krutch, in his book *Experience and Art*, states: "Indeed rival systems have contradicted one another so flatly that it might almost seem as though new groups of critics had set up shop by the simple process of inverting the cardinal doctrine of their competitors, and as though ingenuity had been exhibited chiefly in the discovery of new sets of opposing aims or qualities which could be championed."

Art functionaries serve from a variety of commitments. Some stumble into officialdom through a wholehearted involvement with art experience as both a necessity and a possibility. But there is no point in excusing art functionaries from the bad effects they create on the basis that they are men of reasonable good will. They usually serve to cloud, confuse, and deny the existence of art as an experience. They impose cannons of judgment which are irrelevant to the experience of art. They create hierarchies of excellence which are arbitrary and totally alien to the esthetic moments and deny the public its right to create individual standards geared to individual needs. That is only the beginning of their mischief.

Functionaries, by and large, are unfamiliar with, or largely disinterested in, the esthetic moments that art experience offers. They have other needs to fill which landed them upon the threshold of art. And on the threshold, they will stay as those needs are met. They have jobs to keep, prestige to gain, collections to manipulate, boredom to discourage, services to promote, and sculpture to sell. Their own loss is their own right up to the point where their clamor and ambition pervades and directs the possibility of art experience for others. This it does.

Institutions naturally lend themselves to those who seek power. They provide a recognizable structure from which to launch a career. The wealthy amateur engages at the top through philanthropy, board, fund, and committee work; the expert is on the lower rungs or off by himself free lancing his opinions or his wares. The impresario balances art and entertainment on all levels without a clear idea of any difference. The performer pursues his catch-as-catch-can search for an income in whatever niche he can find, the hobbyists press their work upon a grateful public, and the therapists scale new heights of foundation money for research in all directions.

Where is the object? Carefully housed away where it will do no major harm. It is crammed into a proper context and left there. When the cash register is plugged in the doors will be opened. Where is the viewer? Where he belongs until he is called for. When the bell rings he will be wheeled out to enjoy the show. When it is over he will put himself away. Where is the artist? He has disappeared. But he is not missed. The institution does not require him. History has already furnished too many to keep up with.

Institutions are not inimical to art experience, but art experience itself is not subject to institutionalization. The experience is first and fundamental. The institution could actively support the continuing communication between the creator and the viewer through the object, past and present. But the institution cannot give up its role and arbiter and law giver. It cannot abandon hierarchies of taste and recognize the single continuum of vulgar to rare without stepping in to label any single object as either, or placing it in any way along that continuum. If art experience is to be opened, then it must be opened wide with no strings attached.

Is this to say we are to recognize no objects in the past as being vulgar or rare? How are museums to operate? They would choose objects which were typical using the common materials, tools, content, and techniques of the time. Beyond this, the museum could create a specific value in taste which might represent the best work in its corporate view, but which should *not* be represented as being of great moment to its viewers. Of course, any selection involves an esthetic decision. But a public armed with views and commitments of its own, a public which has been spared the endless cudgeling of museums, teachers, parents, and reviewers would be better equipped to defend itself against a particular bias undertaken by any single museum.

Art cannot have a living place in a culture which is not aware of what art is and what it involves. Our best intentions will lead us astray. The foundations of art must be re-laid. But they cannot be re-laid until we admit all impulses and all sources of response and knowledge as equally valid parts of total mind. That is to say, we must reshape important foundations of our culture to encourage art experience.

Business, government, schools, hospitals, homes and people now live almost completely without art. Would we improve our awareness of life and strengthen our resolve to create a more humane life if we encouraged the sensual-physical responses to engage us on the same level as we admit logical-rational responses? When we look at the culture we have perpetuated, its mechanical blindness and its insistence that progress is defined only on material terms, the answer would seem to be an unqualified, yes.

Often we are told that art thrives. Figures are quoted sighting the number of symphonies, museum attendance, and art auction prices. Religious experience, which in one respect is like art experience, has diminished steadily. Both require commitment, study, and belief. What people really mean is that income is up and the business is thriving. That is, people attend symphonies without hearing the music, take in show they do not see, and live with books they do not understand, even when they read them. The conditioning has been so effective that we may now live with art objects and still remove art experience from our lives. Belief and imagination are held to be childish and primitive traits. WE dare not indulge them. We have changed the whole relationship and still managed to keep up the appearance of a broad vital culture.

The feeling is that if one spends money to support art, that is equivalent to participating in it. But art experience has no direct connection with money. Our association with art cannot be both passive and real. But we are determined to remain uninvolved. The great majority of college graduates leave our institutions of higher learning every year totally untouched by exposure to art. For four years they successfully resisted its seductive presence in the immediate neighborhood. They missed the late coffee talks, the passions of dispute, the exciting tangle of books, ideas, words, lectures, concert, and show hopping and the rest of it. They learned early and refused to indulge themselves. They kept their eyes on the ball and headed unswervingly toward objective goals.

We are engaged in a grand display. The institution has never looked better. The business of art increases. Leisure time sends millions to the canvas and funds raise more and larger buildings in honor of art's place in society. But the flow of communication and money is restricted to the institution and those who serve it or borrow upon it. The viewer is incidental and the artist is out.

To comfort ourselves we encourage the notion that artists are hero-saints. This is a confirmation of our conviction that art experience is separate. The composer, the poet, the playwright, the painter, are paupers. We have cut them off form economic participation. As everyone knows, their work is enough and it is secretly suspected that they rather enjoy the role of the sufferer. How they get their bread is the concern of no one. Only auto workers, salespeople, clerks, city officials, farmers, and miners are subject to such mundane problems. We imagine the artist out adrift on the great sea of art where, somehow without benefit of visible support, he will survive by magic. The institution was built upside down. Last come the makers; the creators who build the catalyst for art experience. First come functionaries, the amateurs, the dilettantes who may, or may not, ever have sensed the necessity and power of art experience.

The cycle goes on from generation to generation. Strangers, odd folk who know and respond to art experience break it momentarily, but they are soon swept into the powerful tide of public mood and are lost from view. In actuality, artists survive, not by pure spiritual acts of will, but by becoming professional applicators to the benefits of public and private charity – by stevedoring, selling shoes, teaching. For their existence rests upon the same vulgar need as all the others. Soon they discover that their primary interest and skill is not saleable enough to count on shoes and bread every month of the year. Like the rest of society they must enter the marketplace on the terms of its demand. Unlike the rest of society, they must stand aside while armies of parasites feast off the work which cannot make them a living.

Is the art experience enhanced by the fact that artists must eat bad food and live in cold houses in sharp contrast to the conditions under which curators, dealers, reviewers, conductors, publishers, directors and others who work at the art trade live? Are we really to accept the shibboleth that artists should necessarily work at other endeavors in order to keep a balance between society's condition and their own vision? What happens to technique? Is it improved by stuffing envelopes or stacking lumber or supervising the creation of endless first year paintings and drawings? We must answer, no. The artist's job of work is to produce art objects. If he works at it half time, he will, not develop his full skill. There is plenty of experience available to keep him aware of society's condition in the ordinary course of daily affairs. There is no more reason for artists to work at truck driving than there is for bond salesmen to work at road construction. But as long as art experience remains separate and apart, we will not be able to recognize that truth.

Under the present conditions of life it would not be possible to say who has it the worst. It was not our intention to add fuel to the fire of romantic pity of the artist's life of neglect and suffering. We all live with that and most of it is imposed by our own consent to ignore alternatives.

The abiding problem is evident. We live in a culture which has encouraged us to deny the value of art experience. With some few exceptions we are obliged to state that we live without art as a part of life's regular and recurrent experience. How the, are we to establish new conceptions which could free us from our own misunderstanding? The traditional answer has been through education. In Western society, in our time, education is conducted primarily through the public school. Therefore, this discussion must include art experience as it applies to that institution.

ART AND THE PUBLIC SCHOOL

The present culture, which has elevated the material-mechanical advantage of man's power over environment and submerged the subjective response we make to that condition and other conditions, is in full swing. We have concretized our approach to new problems and have objectified our lives. We have an old ethos and a full heritage to support and nurture our conviction that science is a single best and sufficient road to truth. Farmers, religionists, shop keepers, brokers, miners, industrialists, and teachers agree that as life becomes increasingly complex, we must increase our effort to seek objectification of it. We must not hesitate, for survival depends upon our adaptability to conform to the dictates science will provide. If we fail to adapt quickly, we will be overwhelmed by those who are more alert. These are the political and social truths which have always arisen as a by-product of the heedless race for 'technological know-how', more power, and more control. They are old truths, but they are infinitely more intense than they ever were before.

But the public recognizes something is wrong. Our alliances fail, our friends and enemies become harder to define, and out production seems impotent when we cope with social problems. Science has provided much. But, how much is enough? Apparently we have just enough production to cause problems and not enough to solve them. We must continue to look to science for our salvation. Will new breakthroughs permit both greater production and greater control of its flow? But then where does one find personal satisfaction in an impersonal and objectified world? Perhaps the science of man and the study of his societies can help to find a direction. Still, something is wrong and the people are in doubt.

The public has gradually been taught to put its faith in science, reserving the right to judge and direct it in a Christian-Judaic context. Intellect and inquiry have not seemed to provide the brighter ground to build upon that the public had hoped for. Science and religion which are traditionally brought forward by the best trained people have resulted in new and visible failures as well as successes.

When people are in doubt, they are thrown back upon visible and objective guides. These tend to be personal and do not take into account larger issues that relate to the decision at hand. Decisions begin to look deceptively simple which are in effect extremely complex. There is, in other words, a ready distrust of those intellectual powers which recognize difficulties, errors, and ambiguities. In times of crises and disappointments, that distrust grows. At present we sense this ambivalence on all sides. Can intelligence be trusted? Have we forgotten God? Would it be better to return to the simple truths of our predecessors? What do scientists know of life?

The disillusionment spreads to all intellectual endeavors, all works of the mind which have no immediate tangible results. It becomes another important facet of the public mood as it confronts all of the problems of education. It adds its weight in the case of art experience to other and deeper prejudices. We cannot expect the public to keep abreast of new developments and possibilities in all the fields of arts and sciences. It is inevitable that disillusionment will seize them and doubt will prevail.

The important thing for us to recognize is that the public has taken a passive stance with respect to scientific, rational, logical benefits. It is Greek to them, but they are ready to put themselves at the disposal of whatever objective goals objective methods arrive at. Their doubt is less unimportant than their faith. Parents want their children to study mathematics and science. They emphasize real results and objective facts; they offer employment opportunities – a very tangible advantage. But the public attitude towards education in the arts is in sharp contrast to that just mentioned. There is a broad mood of overt distrust.

The purpose of education varies with the differences in goals and values of those who create it. But certain elements remain constant. If we take a general view, we can define it as a process where we learn to distinguish the essence of truth from the appearance of truth. It is a continuous search for the "most true". Education involves the presentation of facts and theories about human endeavor. It is a history of ideas, a record of human achievements and failures. Through it we pass on the best information about the past, and create the sharpest critical evaluation of the present which we are able to develop.

There are these main areas of study: study of man and his associates, study of achievements of the mind as these were developed in four major areas (art, philosophy, science, and language), and the training of technicians (trade skills, electronics, research, and laboratory practices). Individual subjects are arranged under these very general headings, according to the goals of each institution.

In practice, education in a democracy is influenced strongly by the public mood, explicitly and implicitly. The public high school represents the closest approximation to the public will that education is subject to. Below it and above it, the public is willing to relinquish more of its rights to professional educators. On the high school level, we find three prominent characteristics which are found in the majority of schools and which take effect on the programs which are offered:

- A reluctance to fund all areas of study with money which is commensurate with current needs and opportunities.
- Neglect of three areas of study (man and his societies, philosophy, and art) because they do not contribute tangibly to progress. They are considered frills worthy only as they may supplement serious studies and help to form a well-rounded, well-adjusted youth.
- An overwhelming of the total educational program by the possibilities of science. Art, beyond the development of performing skills and school entertainment, is not taken seriously. Close association with art is considered morbid. It energizes dark corners of the mind which are better left alone.

These are the conditions we must begin with when we locate the art experience and the study of art as it occurs in public education. The general public, which supports the schools, and the educators and administrators who shape that support, are largely unaware of the possibilities of art experience. In fact, they are predisposed against it by the powerful overt and covert influences of the past and present which we have discussed. Art educators, individuals who, for the most part, have learned the value of esthetic moments, select themselves out of the general population to keep those moments alive through art. But all of their efforts must be embedded within the larger institution of education which is indifferent to, or actively opposed to, the concept of intuitive knowing, hence the serious study of art. The institution holds that art, by itself, is not enough, so they attach alien aims to it. These aims vary with the particular schools, but they are more or less predictable and take the following forms:

- **Art as a therapeutic endeavor.** It is a cathartic which will purge deep loves, hatreds, and frustrations which otherwise might be realized in anti-social behavior. Under this view, it becomes a school policy for the art class to become a dumping ground for students who are not well adjusted to school. It is assumed that the art teacher, by some unknown process, becomes a competent therapist.

- **Art as a hobby or home crafting class**. Here art is put to, what is imagined to be, a practical use. Students learn to make centerpieces for parties, cards and invitations, build models, study draperies and color and fabric, decorate bowls, finish furniture, and create wall hangings and table mats. All of these activities could be reasonable projects. But when offered back to back ad infinitum, they become nothing larger than an extensive program to justify an otherwise unworthy effort. The history of past achievements and classic problems and materials are ignored.

- **Art as a breather course.** Here is conceived as a class where students can relax and get away from the psychological tensions of learning. Those who are carrying a heavy academic load are scheduled in on the assumption that they can still earn credits but do very little work. Poor students who are too little endowed with capacity are placed in the class on the assumption that since nothing is learned there, they will be able to keep up and avoid the disappointments of failure.

- **Art as a school service.** This view holds that all decorating, stage design, invitations, murals, posters, promotional and event materials and outings become the content of an ad hoc art course. All supplies, ideas, and their execution are drawn from its resources. The art program becomes a vast, and usually poverty stricken, commercial graphics center – an arm identified with, but separate from, the formal business of teaching and learning.

- **Art as a professional skills path.** The expectation is that students will learn the various processes of commercial art: catalog and portrait photography, color lithography, computer generated imagery and modeling, silk screen, overlays, half-tones, fashion design, lettering, layout, architectural rendering, illustration, lettering, interior design, furniture construction, copywriting, the psychology of advertising, etc. The course has nothing to do with art experience and everything to do with tools and materials as they can be manipulated for propaganda purposes. Out of an entire class of 35 students, perhaps one, possibly two, will ever apply for a commercial job. But all must be towed along through this technical jungle.

In the high schools, and worse, in the art education literature and teacher training courses, we see any combination of these assumptions providing a foundation upon which classes and entire curriculums are based. The majority pressure is great. Art classes and art education training are subject to the invasion of a mistrusting public and an eager group of art functionaries who are willing to provide goals for the study of art. The art teacher who wishes to acknowledge and protect art experience for his pupils must actively resist the temptation to accommodate ignorance which would prescribe roles, no matter how they deviate from the subject, in order to be a good member of the team. There are times when resolve must be fierce and diplomacy be reduced to its essentials.

Immediately a question asserts itself. Are artists and art teachers to become experts in the sense that they will stand against the public mood and insist on following their own vision of art at the expense of the public which pays their way? They are. First of all, they are experts and should not shy away from calling themselves that, especially in a field where so many amateurs earn that standing. Second, they are hired to do a job they qualify for. If school districts want art teachers to conduct art classes, we must assume they want help in finding art experiences. We must reiterate that the public mood, not the public, is the enemy. It is the job of the artist, by his work, and the art teacher by his, to defy the cycle of perpetual prejudice. If they can demonstrate that art is an experience, rather than an object or an institution, they can interject the possibility of esthetic moments through art.

We must not suppose that people will forever remain ignorant of their sensual, intuitive powers. Instead, we must imagine that such a rediscovery would be a gift for which they would be grateful. Artists and teachers must insist upon whatever tactics and materials and protection from other interests is necessary to carry their work forward. Anything less would not be honest. It is extremely difficult and, in far too many cases, impossible to foster art experiences under the conditions which prevail in public school buildings. Art teachers should be prepared to remove themselves from buildings where art study is not possible, and they should state openly and clearly why they did so. For the moment, let us assume that a call to battle is not necessary and that if it becomes so, all concerned will understand that the enemy is ignorance, not others of reasonable good will with whom one cannot agree.

Public education is a precious institution, but we must agree with Herbert Read's criticism. In *The Forms of Things Unknown*, he writes: "No education is complete that does not incorporate the evidence of art…our whole conception of education has become functional…conceived as serving the provisional interests of a social economy and not as a conquest of reality. Our education is not even scientific in the strict sense, for it is not disinterested. Education today is a system exactly corresponding to the technological organization of our society, and instead of realizing and regretting the enormous limitation that such a system imposes on the development of the human personality, we take pride in the inhuman efficiency of such a machine."

Before leaving this aspect of the topic, there are two points which should be made clear. First, professional art schools and colleges and elementary schools are subject to the same pressures outlined. Despite the lack of intensity of that pressure when it is compared to the high school, they do fall into the same pitfalls. Largely it is accounted for by the fact that art, its meaning, and it elements, have not been carefully examined with a conscious effort to rid that examination of the paraphernalia imposed on it by the institution of art and the art functionaries which it houses. Beyond that, the professional art school has had an additional problem, which is the second point we must take up.

It is the purpose of art schools to provide their students with a saleable line of skills or a full introduction to the possibilities of expression and response which may be embodied in art experience. They may do both, but not at the same time. The difference is dichotomous and is evident in the content of the object.

Commercial art is a phrase used to describe a non-existent thing, or at least, that is the case as long as we agree that art is an experience, not an object. How would one have a commercial art experience or a commercial esthetic moment based on any art object? The phrase is ridiculous. Art experience is not possible except by the sheerest accident of chance, when technique and materials are geared to a content which is propaganda for a particular buying decision or a specific point of view. Pictures may be created and attractive layouts conceived, but the viewer's participation has been denied. There is one pre-ordained conclusion and the viewer may just as well pocket his imagination. The work is not an invitation. It is a command.

Another obvious fault with the term is that it implies non-commercial art. But art objects, objects made and enjoyed as the catalysts of esthetic moments, are bought and sold. They do have an existence, however slim and tentative it may be, in commercial traffic. But the phrase *commercial art* would be just as erroneous and comical if it were applied to them. The phrase *commercial graphics* would serve better to describe work which uses the technical skills of a creator for a prescribed directive.

For a moment let us focus back on art experience and its relationship to teaching and learning in general terms. Education about art lacks an important ingredient – art experience – unless it is predicated on the ground that a viewer must project himself into the object and actively participate in esthetic moments. Without taking this investment into account, education about art becomes irrelevant. It concentrates on tool skills and vocational training. Or, in the other direction, it becomes art for art's sake, only in a precious sense, emphasizing new or old cannons of taste – not as historical facts, but as eternal truths. Finally, under the full weight of public scrutiny, it may sink to the level of a cathartic where it may, like the fountain of youth, mysteriously rejuvenate the maker. In other words, it becomes anything but the study of art experience.

Art begins with the assumption that an intact sensual-physical response to the world is one crucial part of the mind's multifarious processes. Without this, art experience is not possible. Logical and rational approaches to art have their own validity and my yield up valuable information for one sponsoring them. But they do not respond to esthetic moments which depend also upon a deep intuitive body response to the rhythms inherent in the maker's technique as it is resolved in the art object. We may admire art with an incomplete response to it. We may gather learning about it, which by itself, may gratify us. But without admitting our bodies to full participation in the decisions of our lives and our response to its condition, art experience is impossible.

Specifically, all of our senses must be used and respected. Use and respect are not equivalent. Derogation of the latter causes impairment of the former. Our eyes may focus on things we no longer see, our hands touch things we no longer feel, and our ears attend sounds we no longer discriminate. We often hear the phrase at "one with the universe". We use it in jest. But the kernel of irony lying in its vague phraseology is evident. Today we are required to respond more and more attentively to a wider variety of more urgent objective stimulations. Our populations grow, our communications increase, and our cooperation with others becomes more necessary and more complex. We literally spend more time and energy waiting for and initiating signals than was ever necessary before. We are constantly pursuing the facts we must respond to, and more and more those facts must be relayed through others. They tend to reach us in words and numbers. We strive to eliminate error, to get a clear picture and make a clear response. Our eyes and our ears are tuned to formal, unambiguous communications. We learn codes and decipher them rapidly and accurately. Vaguely we wonder where the rest of our responses fit in, but before we can concentrate long on that inquiry, a new interruption takes us back to our "reality".

In other words, we abandon certain sensual skills. Our discriminations become crude instead of refined. We do not feel the paper in our hand. The texture and color and resistance of it no longer counts. We respond only to the symbols on it. They will reveal the next step, tell us what to think about, how to feel, and when to rise and act on some particular physical engagement with our world. The phrase "at one with the universe" comes up and we smile at our own incredibly narrow spectrum of response. But the loss is real. We have cut off whole segments of gratification, sources of interest, great pain and great joy. And it is precisely these which bind us to a sensual identification with life. Rhythm, repetition and variation are felt without our bones and muscles, lungs, and heart. They act on and reactivate rhythmic impulses. But we deny our bodies. We take pills to put us to sleep, pills to keep us awake, and pills to stand the strain while we are awake. For all we care, the sky might just as well be a tent and moon raised and lowered by a string.

Both intellect and emotion are engaged in the art experience. Without either it is inconceivable. Being in full possession of our senses implies respect for their impulses. To reiterate the point, **the first requirement for art experience is full possession of sensual and physical awareness.** It begins, as it ends, with one's own body.

The teacher must emphasize sensual discrimination: textures, colors, shapes, sounds, movements. They must permit students an opportunity to discover differences and similarities. They should offer a variety of materials and a variety of projects which invite exploration, and if necessary, force it. The teacher must make the materials understandable by analyzing the possibilities of manipulation in them and by abstracting those elements which are subject to separate consideration. Also, the teacher should demonstrate and discuss the details of using tools, planning technical strategy, and providing the chance to practice details of the making process. Without reservations and hesitations, the teacher should lay out the facts and practice which can build skills. If the making of art objects is worthwhile, then the skillful making of those objects is essential.

This comes down to one question: does the student know what he is doing? The answer must always be yes. It must be yes, even if a student's compelling urge to make involves them in calling upon a combination of chance and momentary body feel to make their painting with bare feet and orange juice. They must know what the possibilities are and understand the great range between exploration and mastery which carries spontaneity to a dull thud or a ready possibility. They must respect knowing as being both intellectually and intuitively sensed. In many cases, particularly with adults, it is necessary for a teacher to help students see and touch the world around them. This statement appears always to be a little arrogant, but it is not. All of us are inept at things which are unfamiliar unless we possess special talents. Only a few are still able to retain and respond fully to their physical senses without assistance because by and large, that is no longer a survival requirement. Most people are convinced instruments will tell them more. Art teachers serve only to call attention to that which was once intact and then dismissed. There is no magic about it. Students only recapture something vital which they had overlooked.

There is a second assumption of art experience. It is that art experience is worth the commitment. Esthetic moments occur by chance. Many people seem willing to settle for that, feeling that somehow art is contrived and artificial. They are right. What they forget is that art is the only way one person can communicate an esthetic moment to another. Because the event is contrived, art experience is not equivalent to an esthetic moment. It is more. It is human communication which reveals depth of feeling that would otherwise remain unplumbed. Anyone who seeks art experience must do so actively, not passively. They must approach art knowing that it can make a profound contribution to their lives. They must be aware that they must participate in it.

Here again a teacher must draw upon the assumption that a student can understand this and commit himself to it, at least, tentatively. There are no broad influences which encourage and sustain a student who seeks art experience and skills in making art objects. There is no prestige or waiting employment or the approval of family and friends. On the contrary, the interest is often thought to be morbid or pretentious. The pressures weight against it instead of for it, but it is assumed the student can be encouraged to withstand them.

These are the general requirements which must be met before a student is ready to learn or to progress as a learner about art experience. Their implications for the art teacher are clear. But, before leaving this general discussion, we must touch upon one more point.

What of the class on art history or the lecture series on styles, comparisons, or individual artists? Are we to assume that such experiences are not open to esthetic moments, or that students cannot gain an understanding of art experience without actually building work themselves? Yes. These courses are about art objects or about the creators who made art objects, or about the historical context of either or both. They encourage art experience only by exposing viewers to pictures of art objects. This can be useful. But we must remember these approaches may discourage students by providing no clear idea of what art experience involves and by imposing official standards of past and present experts on taste.

There are individuals who never wet their hands in clay, swing a mallet, or hold a brush who instinctively find themselves enmeshed in visual arts. The same holds true in all art endeavors. All of the equipment for appreciation is there and responds readily and easily without any association with the work of making. They are rare.

Most people are not object makers any longer. This, of course, is one of our major problems in encouraging art experience to remain an integral part of life. Most simply respond to art experience in whatever manner their capacity, training and exposure permits. There are, then, two parts to consider in evaluation the non-studio course of study. As we said, art experience is rarely understood and not encouraged. But it can take place simply because the viewer is in proximity to art objects. But, there is nothing inherent in non-studio courses to cause art experience to take place where it would not have otherwise occurred. Making art objects is the surest way to discover and expand art experience, simply because it deeply involves a variety of mind-body responses.

Art experience is possible under startlingly incongruous aegis. We cannot conclude that under the general pressures which discourage education, and the specific pressures which discourage education about art experience, that art experience cannot still be intelligently appraised and occasionally provided. But we must conclude that this is the exception rather than the rule.

It is of little consequence that few artists ever seriously consider the elements of art experience. It is an old, familiar to them, part of living which has become so vital that living would be inconceivable apart from it. But art teachers must examine the elements of that experience. It is necessary since they must talk and write about it so those who are unfamiliar can comprehend it and lay the foundation for their own participation. That is to say that it is no longer natural for everyone. Older adolescents and adults, particularly, must be brought to it with the conscious intent to recapture the possibility of involving themselves. Those who would teach art should not depend on osmosis. Their efforts must be precisely directed, for the membrane is resistant and the long prejudice is deep.

Even where the body and mind are sufficiently respected to lend themselves to sensual-physical apprehension, the motivation of the average public school student is too poor to readily encompass the commitment to art experience. It is a cliché among public school teachers that motivation is the most difficult phase of their work. And so it is. They step into an arena where contempt for art experience holds high ground. The art teacher must expect an uphill engagement.

Public education has made only token room for the visual arts. Unless the public and school administrators are made aware of art experiences, what they involve and how they contribute wisdom and humane perception to society, we cannot expect public education to be an effective tool for re-introducing art experience back into society. To remedy this we must first understand what art experience involves. Second, we must divest ourselves of the huge overburden of unrelated paraphernalia thrust upon public school art classes. Third, we must create individual programs of art which contain consistent efforts to explain art experience and the possibilities of technique. This means we should, without hesitation or embarrassment, teach skills and theory. Under most circumstances this is best done by practice with tools and materials in projects specifically designed to explore the facts of manipulation and the alternatives of ideation. The final effect of guided practice is to sharpen the student's awareness of sensual discrimination and sensual possibility and restore it to its rightful place as an irreplaceable component of creative endeavor.

ART AND MORALITY

People connected with art are a little uncomfortable with the suggestion that art has any special connection to morality. Many examples of visionary attempts to link it with faith, greater good and the development of humane sensibility come to mind. Generally they leave us with a vague feeling that art has a special contribution to make, but the specific portrayal of the good it leads to offends us because it is either too narrow or too mystical. We imagine the thesis is probably right but after finishing the work we cannot imagine how. The chief difficulty seems to be in the natural propensity of those who love art to protect it by enlarging its claims beyond reason.

At the outset of such a chapter as this, it is necessary to disclaim excess by recognizing two things. First, our words are talking around a subjective experience. It varies from individual to individual, culture to culture, and time to time. Nevertheless we will make positive statements about it based on a broad surmise, not subject to proof. While this approach is a necessity in a theoretical exposition, it is fitting to remind ourselves of its condition at the point where we undertake to reexamine art experience and comment on the current state of Western civilization and to project broad possibilities which art may contribute to society.

Second, it is a simple matter to draw up a list of complaints and lay them at the door of a single circumstance. That problem is compounded when we speak of such a general topic as contemporary Western civilization. The temptation is to use a broad sword in all directions. Here we must make it clear that the conditions which led to the denigration of intuition supersede and overshadow the final effect on art experience. As we mentioned, there is more than one cause which created our image of a divided mind and more than one cause which subsequently strengthened that division. But, our primary concern has been to describe the elements of art experience. As we have seen, art experience itself is only a part of a broader experience, that of the esthetic moment. And the esthetic moment in, in turn, only one of life's many possibilities. When we discuss art we do so with a full recognition that it is a single segment of the experience people may avail themselves of.

Once we make this clear we may proceed to evaluate art experience with proper respect for its full powers. They are great and they are unique. Art experience will not, by itself, resurrect and improve a failing culture, but it can contribute an asset without which an improved culture is not likely to be possible.

In *Defense of Poetry*, Shelley says that "a man to be greatly good, must imagine intensely and comprehensively; he must put himself in place of another and of many others; the pleasures and pains of his species must become his own."

Melvin Rader, in *A Modern Book Esthetics,* writes: "The work of art is objective and yet is dyed with emotion and sensuality. It radiates spiritual expressiveness and is thus a link between mind and mind itself. Art is the only language whereby we can **vividly** transmit our values to others. It breaks down the walls between human beings, and is thus a great solvent of conflict and selfishness. By means of art, the solitudes flow together; love and imaginative understanding become possible."

If these statements accurately reflect the power of art experience to unite people, the question which naturally follows is, how? The answer lies primarily in our understanding of, and appreciation for, subjective knowing.

Our first state, that of infancy, is sensual, physical and subjective. From the first moments of life society must begin to transmit its requirement that we accept common goals and commonly approved objectively determined rules of procedure which will lead to a willingness to cooperate. Rational and logical approaches must displace intuitive and subjective impulses. In order to make the gains society offers us we give up much, voluntarily and by force, of the immediate respect for, and responses to, our own sensations: those which emanate from our sensual awareness and the imagery it sets off. We learn to set these aside as trivial matters which have no importance when compared with the information passed on to us by the tribe. We literally buy our individual response to our own sensibilities to the exact degree that we become skillful in objectively manipulating the environment around us. When we are cold we do not cry out, curl up to conserve our body heat and endure the imagery that state brings about. We turn a dial to raise the temperature or look for a coat which we remember hangs in a certain place or we go indoors or choose a warmer room. The rational processes offer a marvelous lever. It is society's gift to the individual. Learning and memory intervene and we enjoy a higher level of efficiency in managing our affairs. We still feel the cold, just as we still feel joy and rage and hunger. But our response to it is objectified. We reduce the response to one phase of experience - the intuitive feeling which says "I am cold", not "it is cold" – a response in and of itself which sets off a rapid charge of imagery and sensation. We know it is not efficient to stand idly ruminating about a train of thought started by being cold when a simple act will bring immediate satisfaction.

Subjective knowing is often inappropriate. We consider that we can live better and more efficient lives without it. The real difficulty is that we can, but only up to a point. That is to say that logical decisions cannot serve alone, effectively, in all matters. Putting on a coat or adjust a thermostat is not a simple matter when we attend to its secondary effect, for the secondary effect is a tendency to give up our intuitive response altogether. Habit is strong, and cumulative social pressures mold us to the objectivity society needs. This is where displacement occurs. Instead of spending time responding to our deepest urges of pain, joy, hunger, frustration, and satisfaction, we quickly ameliorate them. If experience could be conceived as a continuous graph of emotions with high peaks and sharp depressions, we would see the extremes being lopped off. The graph would be truncated to a narrower range of emotional responses, one geared to the middle range of sensual experience which our rational efforts have made available. We no longer need to go outdoors to feel temperature. We can utilize devices to gauge it and prepare ourselves in advance. In summer, we can activate an air conditioner before discomfort arrives. The point is that, physically, we feel less. Our manipulations can be distilled from symbols.

The tendency to disregard intuitive imaginings moves to another effect – this the most serious one: we use our body's physical senses less and less. We do not need to feel, taste, smell, see and hear wherever we rely on instruments and symbols to accurately give us the information we need in order to proceed. The advantage of objective knowing is obvious, but a nagging question remains – accurate for whom? Will we need a coat if the wind is down and the sun is out? Will we need a coat if we did not skip a heavy breakfast, or if we will be engaged in physical work? Will everyone need a coat under the same conditions? Only our own sensations can supply the answer. In other words, until objective knowledge is perfect and can account for all possible factors under all possible conditions, we cannot rely utterly upon it, and it alone, to guide us even in simple matters. But from all sides we hear advice based upon the assumption that all people are alike and respond alike to the world which surrounds them.

Gradually we have given up much of both aspects of subjective knowing: the act of physically sensing firsthand the state of nature as it is variously found, and the act of responding to such sensations from the confines of one's own privacy without the guilt of seeming foolish and the risk of making errors. For centuries, what we have assumed to be an inevitable conflict has been compounded by the advent of a religious belief which added moral sanction to denial of the body by holding that it is a vehicle of temptation conceived in sin.

By denying a large share of subjective knowing and by supporting a culture which demands that we must deny more, we trade our individuality, our subjective awareness, for efficiency and objective awareness. We assume that objectivity and society must always be pitted against subjectivity and individuality, and until we recreate a culture capable of honoring both, presumable this will continue to be the case. The example of feeling cold and responding to that sensation quickly and effectively is relatively unimportant when compared with other discriminations and the response we could make to them. But even in such a trivial case we can see the defects of a decision intended to be based purely on logic.

To know our world deeply we must know ourselves deeply. We must make a full response to life. We now appear to view people as empty receptacles which, in childhood, stand in neat rows waiting to be filled with a particular formula of evidence, opinions, manners, and ethics up to an imaginary line of adult status. We offer the nourishment as if convinced that no individual emotional components are involved. Evidence to the contrary throws us off balance and we summon an expert to determine how the extremity may be adjusted. But the curiosity of people surely extends to themselves and despite however solemnly we overtly or covertly agree to banish intuition from the honorable realms of mankind's endeavor, its flames eventually will demand an adjustment.

Art experience serves as a fundamental balance wheel. It is a dynamic example of the unity of mind, and the unity of mind and body. Art objects invite a whole response. They keep it alive against the tyranny of excess and denial. But the object is helpless without a willing viewer; without a person who is conversant with the miracle of their own senses and deeply aware of the excitement and opportunity of their own imaginings. Art experience appeals directly to the body through rhythm. Its repetitions and variations reflect the flow of change and the continuous imbalance or order and chaos. Rhythm permits us to sense the particular and the universal in the same instant. It penetrates to the most true. Above all it requires awareness of one's own physical existence which is necessary for a full response.

When we look at the societies of mankind, there are certain things we understand immediately. Rational conceptions, divorced from any deep subjective awareness of existence, generate the prejudices which separate people. A person caught up in the wonder of being alive cannot willingly hurt or follow the order to hate another man he does not know. He is too involved with his own life to disrespect another's. But those who are ignorant of all but the rudest concerns for acquiring bread or who never have had the opportunity to subjectively and freely question all aspects of their own experience cannot be expected to appreciate their involvement with life. On the contrary, life would seem desperate and mechanical to them.

Of all the experiences we contrive, art offers the richest spectrum for the play of a total response. It opens an experience limited only by the skill and insight of a creator and the imagination and experience of the viewer. For a moment there is respite from the rule of right and wrong. One person's hands, body, or mind invites another to share in a full understanding of a single fragment from life's wide sea. When we develop a total response, we increase our sensitivity to life around us; responding fully, we know ourselves fully. Knowing ourselves fully, we know others.

The intuitive knowing found in the esthetic moment art experience offers, generates sympathy and compassion. It provides a total framework from which we may order priorities – a moral perspective. We come to know, even from the darkest and most violent struggles an art object may carry, that full expression of the miracle of life always calls forth our respect for it. We see new possibilities, some terrible and some sublime, but all warmed by the heart and hand of another whose compassion and respect required him to speak fully, at least once. This is the how of art's moral involvement. It binds us together as no other experience ever can. We cannot afford to live without art.

In his book *Venture to the Interior*, Laurens Van der Post writes: "The world to my mind has never been fuller of finer thinking than it is today. I never pick up a paper, magazine, or book, be they in Japanese, French, Javanese, Russian, English or Tai, and fail to be struck by the fine thoughts, the idealistic feelings, the noble sentiments they express. Yet, though all the contributing writers appear to be merchants of man's finest feelings, has there ever been an age that, considering its lights, has done worse things than this one, with its class hatreds, race hatreds, color prejudices, world wars, and concentration camps? Has there been another age, that knowing so clearly the right things to do, has so consistently done the wrong ones?"

We do know better. But how we know is as important as what we know. Objective knowing, by its' own nature, is dispassionate and uncommitted. For it to be otherwise would be a contradiction of its terms of existence. This is its limitation as well as its virtue. Just knowing is not enough. We need to recognize and encourage subjective knowing as well as objective knowing to enjoy a full response to our existence and to create a moral perspective.

It is not possible to achieve the full measure of an educated mind until we create an inner life which orders and nourishes our perspective, our sense of responsibility. We actively create it. Simply waiting for it to overtake us with the same passive faith we submit to while waiting for a bus will not do. We cannot arrive at a point where we are familiar with the objective facts of our existence and the subjective possibilities of sympathy and commitment without knowing any of the details of both. It is necessary to build an inner life with the same care one builds a house to live in, for this, in fact, is what it is. For the reasons described earlier, there is today an ill wind abroad which equates spirit and fulfillment with tangible accomplishment. It adapts an action process of utter passivity which hurls one into the maelstrom of raw experience protected by nothing larger than good intentions. Adequate for a soldier of fortune, perhaps, but not for people who would build shelter for themselves and others, not shelters to which one crawls to permanently withdraw from the rude tumble of life, but places of refuge where the spirit may take high ground to reconsider before launching out once more into the active muddle of affairs. An inner life requires preparation and sacrifice. There is no other way to build it than piece by piece as imagination, study, and experience provide its materials.

The problems we face embody in their existence, and in the way we discuss them, a commitment to non-sensual life goals. We see monstrous contradictions of moral principle being ignored because people have risen above their bodies. We no longer recognize the urgency of hunger and cold and pain. From the narrowed middle of experience the worst agony is boredom and uninvolvement. Art experience keeps involvement alive. It reveals the insights which widen our perspective by appealing to the deepest, earliest and most urgent sensations of being alive which we possess. It gives rise to feelings not capable of moral compromise. It honors existence and all things which protect it and recognizes all things which threaten existence as products of petty, selfish, or incomplete responses to life.

Since we have denied the value of intuition and even consider our body sensations to be a clarion cry from Hell, we have cut ourselves of and risen above our bodies. We have removed, or at the least greatly reduced the most urgent and direct source of sympathy and compassion available to us. All the bright decorator colors, and all of the books on the naturalness of sex and the joys of outdoor living cannot disguise the fact the actual experience of feeling alive has become so abstract and non-sensual that we hold hunger and killing to be reasonable tools of a moral foreign policy and view unemployment and poverty as natural by-products of a prosperous society. Also in our own country we watch unmoved while the entire industry of advertising appears to promote fear, anxiety and dissatisfaction in order to sell merchandise. It spreads a plague through our land as dangerous as global warming. It gives shape to our terrors and creates our children's aspirations. It undermines joy and confidence. Yet we look upon that industry as a leader in the search for prosperity.

It is true that if we guide our society on only logical, pragmatic premises, we do not encounter moral contradictions, for moral commitment is then reduced to the least terms of expediency. But on the same ground the neat surgery that separates morality from the great survival issues, simply because we do not face them on a day to day basis, fails. Not only do they still remain, but their pressure increases. It is apparent that either we make an adequate response of a total reply or we submit to whatever disasters apathy and special interest concoct. This choice is in doubt.

Of course our difficulties have many faces and require complicated, delicate, and energetic solutions. Art experience will probably contribute nothing directly to the economic wellbeing of Appalachian miners or Chinese farmers. Its contribution lies only in sensitizing people, making them more aware of the value or existence and creating a moral perspective to order priorities at the service of protecting the miracle of life.

How can we suppose a single dance, a painting, a pot, a play, a musical passage, a short story to directly play a part to improve people's sensibilities when we admit as many art experiences as viewers can find, and assume a nearly unlimited range of objects to stimulate and satisfy the viewers? Does a vulgar or common object, so considered by an experienced and thoroughly trained viewer, contain the same possibility for stimulation and satisfaction as a rare art object? For a moment, let us return to the original definition of art given earlier: art is an esthetic experience under particular and specific conditions. It takes place when a viewer invests in an object, made for the occasion of such an experience, with their own imagination and senses new possibilities about the condition of their existence. It is a sensed imagery, intuition and rationality forming a momentary order of new understanding.

We see that the answer must be qualified by two observations. First, every viewer's response for all practical purposes of discussion, must be separate and unique, that is, it is based on his own experience and imagination. Therefore, strictly speaking, we cannot say that one or many objects ever contain the same possibility of stimulation and satisfaction for one or many viewers. In fact, we surmise that it must be true that no one ever responds to the same object in an esthetic moment in the same way twice. We must assume that changes occur in a viewer, over time, which are sufficient to alter his experience. We know that the object which once failed to invite an esthetic moment will be able to do so in the future, and the converse also holds true.

The second qualifier is that we must not confuse entertainment with art experience. The former is passive, merely a passing of time in amusement and diversion. The second is active, requiring imaginative participation. The dividing line depends upon the individual involved, but in the main, it seems apparent that most of the economic traffic alleged to flow into and through the institution of art buys entertainment, not art experience. In other words, when we speak of common art objects we are probably excluding most popular recordings, at least most of the time, and most popular singers, most of the time. Yet we recognize that art experience does flow from such performances for some viewers and we should be grateful for it.

Art experience is always valuable. It pushes out old walls and looks beyond what we had sensed to be a limitation. We are not precisely the same after it as we were before. No matter how we may retreat from its new possibilities, the effects of the actual encounter remain. Any extension of sensibility is worthwhile. If it occurs through the catalyst of art we consider vulgar, we should honor it, not despise it. Regardless of how we view it, an object which earns any viewer's contribution of final form serves art and people by providing art experience.

Another point arises which we cannot dismiss. As we have mentioned earlier, one important variant in the artist's work of making is his conceptualization of content. We have considered it carefully in connection with the understatement and the viewer's role as it applies to that condition. It appears possible that the judgment we make of vulgar and rare quality relates directly to the content's degree of understatement. This surmise is based on the importance of experience with objects as a factor in changing taste. The more practiced and familiar we are, the less help we need in clues, guides, and information.

We can speculate that an object which leaves enough room in its statement for an experienced viewer might appear empty to one needing more signs of familiar ground. On the other hand, the experienced viewer might consider an object suitable for a younger or less practiced viewer gaudy, busy, or tending toward a pat solution. The continuum would stretch from a complete statement allowing no participation and no art experience to a reduction where no conception is apparent, also allowing no participation or art experience. But we must add that since we cannot make a negative statement universal, that chance could operate to make any art object, no matter how extreme or badly conceived and build, serve as the catalyst for an art experience. In such a case, no matter how inconceivable it might seem, art's contribution is made and a small advance toward subjective knowing and a moral perspective is made.

The question, how is it possible for someone who responds to vulgar objects or art to create a moral perspective and lend themselves to a more humane society, is not the question we should ask. The real question is, how long will we permit the institution of art and its art functionaries to take the lead in imposing false standards of excellence, standards which have no relevance to the experience of art, upon children and a passive public? This influence is a formidable tool against an unsophisticated person's recognition of the value of his own feelings in making esthetic decisions. It acts to deny their participation in art experience. It tells them their feelings are silly and foolish because they derive from things museums would never hang nor reviewers comment upon.

Beyond that there is the larger question: how are we to maintain art experience and seek sustenance and perspective from its contributions when society as a whole has mistaken the appearance for the essence and unleashed all its power, from the loftiest ramparts of business, government and the pulpit to scourge sensitivity and intuition from participation in shaping society? Before that massive battery art experience is, indeed, small. Without the perspective of art experience our culture will probably fail, but it is not aware of this and seems determined to bury art in the name of art, under the deluge of greater museums, longer grants, wealthier committees, and more officials to challenge and harass art's bright possibility.

The look and sound of words strung logically together to rationally describe life cannot begin to express the feelings we have about it. A grunt or a scream might serve better. But we pretend we are beyond all that. The assumption is that symbols and abstractions will distill the essence by eliminating the emotion. That is to say that we are beyond ourselves. By leaving our bodies behind we hope to step into a new dimension of possibilities. Above all we do not grunt or scream. We know we are beyond that and must not give way to ourselves.

On all sides the sense of being alive and being aware of that as separate from not being alive is diminished. We are as embarrassed by our own extremes of feeling as a child who makes a faux pas at table with guests, and for the same reason. We also hunger for connection, affection, identity, something vital to cling to and think about. Our hunger escapes our control. The ragged and unvarnished truth is out. We are caught right in the middle of ourselves without the slightest chance of a polite pretense. Still we must not scream or grunt. We may talk about life but we must never unbolt the dark evidence that we have it. We stand awkwardly feeling the surge of our own blood.

But, we are not beyond ourselves. We cannot choose to ride above life like a cork on a pond. It is in us and we are in it. We have the opportunity to sense it fully and draw our strength from that acceptance. Life is not utterable but art offers a vantage point from which we may find, in the instant of its experience, a full recognition and a whole participation. Art takes over the impulse of a scream, laughter, joy, tears, or a grunt. It transforms these fragment particulars of emotional energy into a sustained object which will tell and retell something of the incredible variety and possibility which the joy and agony of being alive presents.

If life is unutterable, art experience confronts us with that central fact of our condition. It arms us against the foibles of the grand plan, and disarms us that we may accept the tentative, hopeful, and unspoken reaching of a being's seeking to find unity with themselves and others. It is a testimony to high purpose and intelligence that humanity could create such a sympathetic and compassionate way of expressing joy and agony, that this expression would open new possibilities.

But the consensus is strong. We feel compelled to rise above life and gain mastery over it. We want only to divide and analyze. To the last person we will play the game of strategy and objective management, oblivious to the denial of our body's subjective report. Our inaccuracies haunt us. We cannot trust ourselves and certainly we cannot trust others. Life is a disease which we must control. The taste, smell, look, feel, and sound of it must be subordinated to objective knowing and material manipulation. We will take ourselves in hand and put our faith into the science of living and our energy into the frenzy of progress. The darkness will pass and we will finally utter life with clarity and precision. Chaos and want will disappear.

But art experience says, "Beware!" Life is in us, large, awful, and unutterably possible. It is both objectively and subjectively real, sustained for each, primarily by the conception each of us has of it. We need not waste the earth to improve it. Art experience calls us instead to heed the cries of visceral exultation, humor, and despair which link us together. It teaches that we cannot appraise our condition intelligently until we respect the possibilities each one of us endures and protect our search to give back to all of us something from the perspective of our own sensibility.

*

About the Author

ALAN D RILEY was born in West Virginia but was raised in Minnesota. At age 17, he joined the marines. He later attended the University of Minnesota, where he completed his MA while working as a group worker at a settlement house.

Alan moved with his wife to Seattle in 1960 to embark on a career as an art teacher. Eventually he returned to the field of social work as a researcher for United Way, and the moved to the Model Cities program as an administrative assistant. Following that, he became a consultant in social services management.

Early in his career Alan also became engaged in three deep interests: wildlife conservation, peace action, and civil rights issues. These passions led to board assignments, state task forces, and governor's commissions in these areas. Throughout these many life endeavors, Alan's work as an artist and poet endures. He now resides in Kenmore, Washington, in perpetual "unretirement".

www.ingramcontent.com/pod-product-compliance
Lightning Source LLC
Chambersburg PA
CBHW070208230526
45471CB00002B/872